A HISTORY OF ASTROLOGY

DEREK & JULIA PARKER

ANDRE DEUTSCH

This book was designed and produced by
The Oregon Press Limited,
Faraday House, 8–10 Charing Cross Road,
London WC2H 0HG

First published in 1983 by
André Deutsch Limited,
105 Great Russell Street,
London WC1

ISBN 233 97576 4

Design: Gail Engert
Picture research: Anne-Marie Ehrlich
Reader: Raymond Kaye

Colour plates printed by Acorn Typesetting and
Litho Services Limited, Feltham, Middlesex, England
Filmset, printed and bound by Butler and Tanner Limited,
The Selwood Printing Works, Frome, Somerset, England

HALF-TITLE A 19th-century Venetian decorative Zodiac

FRONTISPIECE 'An allegory of astrology', an 18th-
century tribute to the part astrology played in the
development of geography, the making of a modern
calendar, and the exploration of terrestrial phenomena

CONTENTS

FOR JONATHAN

ILLUSTRATION SOURCES

INTRODUCTION

There are two major problems to be faced when writing about the history of astrology. One is that of length. Astrology has been of great importance in many countries of the world since long before the invention of writing, and until at least the end of the 16th century; recently there has been a considerable revival of interest. The amount of documentation is therefore almost incalculable, and to examine the subject in depth would mean a work of such size that probably no publisher could contemplate it without a massive subsidy, and only a writer prepared to give his life to the subject could attempt it.

The second problem is that of partiality. Very few people seem able to discuss astrology without emotion. This is partly a matter of temperament, but also often a matter of misinformation and almost always of bias of one sort or another. It can be, for instance, the result of a simple contemplation of the harm that may be done by an uncritical belief in the infallibility of astrological advice – quite as much harm as can be done by the uncritical acceptance of the infallibility of theological advice. Sometimes too a simple-minded devotion to astrology has resulted in the acceptance of legends entirely without basis, invariably supporting the claims of astrology. Some 'histories' have repeated such legends. In a recent one by an American writer, for example, it is asserted that Lord Byron was 'quite a good astrologer, who set up his own son's chart and quite accurately predicted the main events of the latter's life.' This would be a more convincing statement if Byron had ever had a son, or if there was the faintest evidence anywhere in his life or letters that he was even slightly interested in astrology.

The present authors should declare an interest. Julia Parker is a consultant astrologer, past President of the Faculty of Astrological Studies, founded in London in 1948, with pupils in most countries of the world, and co-author of *The Compleat Astrologer*, a comprehensive textbook of astrology. Derek Parker, the other co-author, remains a sceptic for whom the practice of astrology is largely a mystery, but who has become convinced that there is sufficient evidence now available to support many astrological propositions, and that it would be foolish to dismiss the subject out of hand.

In this book we have attempted to maintain a reasonable balance. This is not meant to be a work that will convince anyone that astrology works, or that it does not. It is meant as a necessarily brief account of the spread of astrology through the civilized world, and of the major figures involved in its history.

Amid the shelves of bad books on the subject, there are a few important and reliable source books to which any writer about astrology must be indebted. Lynn Thorndike's massive *History of magic and experimental science* (1941) is most certainly one. Jack Lindsay's *Origins of astrology* (1971), F. H. Cramer's *Astrology in Roman law and politics* (1954), and Keith Thomas's *Religion and the decline of magic* (1971) are other examples; and A. L. Rowse's *Simon Forman* (1974) is the earliest example of the work of a serious historian who has thought it worth while to go through the untouched papers of a prominent Elizabethan astrologer. Dr John Dee's papers await similarly thorough treatment from some adventurous Elizabethan scholar. Finally, no reader can be thoroughly versed in the latest state of astrology who has not read Geoffrey Dean's and Arthur Mather's *Recent advances in natal astrology* (1977); while the work of the husband and wife team, Michel and Françoise Gauquelin, in several volumes, provides much statistical evidence, and thought-provoking argument. The work of Dane Rudhyar in America and of John Addey of the British Astrological Association is more specialized still, and the journals of the British Association and the American Federation of Astrologers are serious publications worth examination.

We are grateful, as always, to various librarians for their assistance; and to many astrologers who have been quick with suggestions of material to be consulted. And we are grateful to the Folio Society Limited for permission to quote lines from William Ginnis's translation of Sebastian Brant's *The ship of fools*, and to Penguin Books Limited for permission to quote from Nevill Coghill's 'translation' of Chaucer's *The Canterbury tales* (© 1958, 1960, 1975, 1977).

DP
JP

I

DISTANT BEGINNINGS

How, where, when, did astrology originate? How, where, when, why did man first begin to believe that the Sun, Moon and visible planets influence his character and life, the health of his beasts, the quality of his crops, the weather – indeed, every aspect of life on earth?

The answer must be, almost as soon as he was capable of intelligent thought, for he then realized that the Sun as a source of warmth and light ruled all living things; that with the Moon the tides swelled and sank, that it affected other natural cycles, that it had an effect upon emotional stability. Here was the basis of an astrological theory. Interestingly, some of the earliest astrological artifacts to have survived come from the Middle East where, in about 15,000 BC, the earliest agricultural systems evolved – gardeners have always recognized that there is a difference between the quality of morning and afternoon light, and that the times at which plants are planted, herbs picked, seem to affect their growth and virtue.

On the whole, it must have been man's natural reverence for the magical, strange moving lights in the sky, regarded as gods, that led to the development of astrology. Out of the thick mists that conceal the earliest history of the subject have come down to us a number of cuneiform tablets – brick and stone slabs inscribed with triangular or wedge-shaped characters – recording the very simplest astronomical phenomena: eclipses of the Moon, certain planetary movements, interpreted as predicting famine or war or peace or plenty.

Babylonia during the 18th-17th centuries BC was very riddled with

superstition, and many omens were used and recorded – the bites of certain animals, dreams, patterns of bird flight, the appearance of newborn babies ('When a woman bears a child with small ears, the house will fall into ruin'), and such eccentricities as the appearance in one's house of a pig with palm fibres in its mouth. Astronomical phenomena were only one aspect of man's attempts to predict the future, but a very widespread one: an interest in the earliest form of astrology was common to several early civilizations, not only in the Middle East, from Anatolia to Persia, but in the Far East and in the Incan, Mayan and Mexican civilizations, where those planets that could be seen by the naked eye – Mercury, Venus, Mars, Jupiter and Saturn – were identified as gods with various names and personalities, and where their movements against the background pattern of the stars were regarded as obviously significant.

Astronomer-astrologers slowly acquired more and more knowledge about the planets, and began not only to observe eclipses but the way in which the planets moved – sometimes hesitating, sometimes appearing to move backwards, sometimes seeming to meet each other, then part; as they did so, they elaborated the predictions they based on the movements. Only the roughest forecasts were being made in the time of Ammisaduqa, tenth king of the First Dynasty, in the 17th century BC, but royal libraries of the Assyrian kings at Nineveh, Calah (Nimrud) and Ashur in the 8th–7th centuries BC, and the temple libraries of the chief cities of Babylon, had on their shelves a collection of over 7000 astrological omens recorded on 70 tablets (now known, after the opening words of the first omen, as *Enuma Anu Enlil*).

The reason why this elaboration of the astrological theory took place in the Middle East rather than, say, among the American Indians of

Probably the earliest extant horoscope, drawn up for a child of the Seleucid era in Syria (*c* 200 BC), a period during which astrologers began to work for individuals rather than for the state alone. The predictions were rough and ready: 'The place of Venus means wherever he may go it will be favourable; he will have sons and daughters ... The place of Mercury means the brave one will be first in rank, he will be more important than his brothers'

A tablet from Babylon, *c*700 BC, recording astronomical observations of the movements of Venus. These were set down not because of any interest in the construction of the solar system, but in order to attempt to discover the 'meaning' of sky phenomena

A Babylonian tablet of c870 BC shows Shamash, the Sun god, seated in his shrine. Two servants hold a symbol of the Sun in place while a priest and a goddess usher a king into Shamash's presence. Inside the shrine, above the Sun god's head, are symbols of the Moon, Sun and goddess Ishtar (the planet Venus). Shamash, in the treaties of the time, was represented as the Judge; the Moon, which 'illuminated heaven and earth', was invoked to inflict leprosy and desolation on the enemies of the treaty maker; while Venus, should the enemy refuse to respect the treaty, would 'cause your wives to lie in the bosoms of your enemies before your eyes . . .'

Babylonian boundary stones (this is one of *c* 12 BC) often show representations of a scorpion. This may be an astrological symbol of Scorpio, established early as the sign of war. It is possible, however, that the scorpion may simply symbolize a curse (directed at those who ignore the boundary). At the top of this stone, however, are other astrological symbols

Wisconsin or among the Aztecs, who certainly had an equally keen early interest in the subject, was that the Babylonians were better astronomers and mathematicians; they evolved a calendar, and by 500 BC were already moving towards the invention of the zodiac, that essential element in the personalization of astrology.

The Babylonians puzzled for centuries over the patterns in the night sky before producing a calendar reliable enough to enable them to predict eclipses and to work 'backwards' in order to figure out the celestial events of the past. They seem to have started by simply working out the duration of day and night, then of the rising and setting of the Moon and the appearance and disappearance of Venus. The very earliest calendars date a new month from the first appearance of a new Moon. But the fact that the interval between new Moons is irregular – on average, 29 days, 12 hours, 44 minutes and 3 seconds – meant that it was extremely difficult to devise a calendar in which each month began with the new Moon, but each year began at the spring equinox. (To do so, you have to declare an extra month every two or three years – and even then you will be one and a half days out every eight years.)

The details of early calendars and their evolution are complex; suffice to say that the problem was solved with reasonable accuracy (and, let us remember, without the aid of mechanical clocks) by the Babylonians. Since then, there have been additional complications and evolutions. Julius Caesar had to summon an astronomer from Alexandria to sort out the muddle into which the Roman calendar degenerated, and his Julian calendar eventually fell out of phase by no less than eleven days, so that in 1752 Britain was forced to adopt the Gregorian calendar (established in the rest of Europe by Pope Gregory in 1582), cutting eleven days from the year. At midnight on 2 September came 14 September, and people rioted in the streets because they thought the civil servants were doing them out of eleven days of life.

Once a calendar had been devised, observation and the application of mathematics meant that planetary movements could be predicted. The next step was the invention of the zodiac.

In the first place this was devised as a means of measuring time. It is a circle around which twelve constellations are set, each marking a segment of thirty degrees of the ecliptic, the imaginary path the Sun seems to follow on its journey round the earth. Because that journey takes more or less 365 days, astronomers in Babylon, Egypt and China independently arrived at the idea of dividing the ecliptic into 360 degrees, easily divisible into twelve sections.

The circle, for practical purposes, had to start somewhere. In ancient times it started variously from certain fixed stars – from Aldebaran or the Bull's Eye, for instance, or from Regulus, the brightest star in Leo. In modern astrology it starts from the vernal equinox – the point at which the Sun seems to cross the equator from south to north at the spring equinox of the northern hemisphere on 20, 21 or 22 March each year.

But the equinox not only never occurs in the same spot for two years running, but its place slowly seems to rotate around the sky, taking about 28,800 years to complete the circuit (a phenomenon known as Precession of the Equinox). This is because the Earth, as it rotates, wobbles like a top slowing down; the Pole thus describes a circle, moving backwards through the zodiac. Similarly, if the zodiac is measured from a fixed point (say the first degree of Aries), *it* moves slowly backwards. However, this is the system used by most modern astrologers; it is known as the tropical zodiac. Some astrologers, like the ancients, use the fixed or sidereal zodiac, measured from the stars (not as fixed as all that, however, for it too moves – by one day in every 72 years!).

THE SIGNS COMPARED

	Babylonia	China (equivalent months)	India/Greek	Sanscrit
ARIES	hunga *(hireling)*	ch'un fên *(vernal equinox)* ch'ing ming *(clear and bright)*	Krios	Mesha *(Ram)*
TAURUS		ku yü *(grain rains)* li hsia *(summer begins)*	Tauros	Vrisha *(Bull)*
GEMINI	mastabba.galgal *(great twins)*	hsiao man *(grain fills)* mang chung *(grain in ear)*	Didumoi	Mithuna *(couple)*
CANCER		hsia chih *(summer solstice)* hsaio shu *(slight heat)*	Karkinos	Karkata *(Crab)*
LEO	ur.gul.la *(lion)*	ta shu *(great heat)* li ch'iu *(autumn begins)*	Leōn	Simha *(Lion)*
VIRGO	ab.sin *(furrow)*	ch'u shu *(limit of heat)* pai lu *(white dew)*	Parthenos	Kanya *(Virgin)*
LIBRA	zibanitu *(horn, later scales)*	ch'iu fên *(autumn equinox)* han lu *(cold dew)*	Zugos *(yoke)*	Tula *(Balance)*
SCORPIO	gir.tab *(scorpion)*	shuang chiang *(hoar-frost descends)* li tung *(winter begins)*	Skorpion	Vrischika *(Scorpion)*
SAGITTARIUS	PA.BIL.SAG *(?)*	hsiao hsüeh *(little snow)* ta hsüeh *(heavy snow)*	Toxotēs *(archer)*	Dhanus *(Bow)*
CAPRICORN	suhur.mas *(goat-fish)*	tung chih *(winter solstice)* hsiao han *(little cold)*	Aigokerōs *(goat-horned)*	Makara *(Sea-monster)*
AQUARIUS	GU.LA *(giant?)*	ta han *(severe cold)* li ch'un *(spring begins)*	Hydrokhoös *(water-pot)*	Kumbha *(pot)*
PISCES	zibbati *(tails)*	yu shui *(rain water)* ching chih *(excited insects)*	Ikhthues	Mina *(Fish)*

Plus

	Babylonia
Pleiades	zappu *(tuft of hair)*
Hyades	Gu.an.na *(bull of heaven)*
Orion	Sib.zi.an.na. *(shepherd of heaven)*
Perseus	Sugi *(charioteer*
Aurige	gamlu *(scimitar)*
Praesepe	la.lul *(crab?)*
southern fish	sim.mah *(great swallow)*
northern fish	aninitum *(a goddess)*

The Precession of the Equinox presents astrologers with a problem. Aldebaran, on 15 degrees of Taurus in ancient times, has now moved forward so that it is on 8 degrees of Gemini, and someone born with the Sun in Taurus centuries ago might well be born in 1985 with the Sun in precisely the same spot relative to the Earth, but be in popular parlance 'a Geminian' rather than 'a Taurean'. Throughout the ages critics have used this as a weapon against astrologers, without realizing that it is only popularly that astrology has anything to do with the constellations, 'the stars' as astrology columnists put it. Astrologers are, with a few exceptions, concerned with the movements of the Sun, Moon and planets within the solar system, describing these in terms of their background. That background may change, but the planets' positions relative to Earth (all that matters) will not.

For some time it was believed that the zodiac as we know it originated in Babylon. More recently, it has become clear that it is the product of Babylonian, Egyptian and Assyrian astronomy. The Ram, for instance, the symbol of Aries, is of Egyptian origin; Taurus, the Bull, originated in Babylon, where it was called Gud.anna. Leo, the Lion, is Egyptian (in Babylon the same constellation figure was called the Great Dog). Some signs sprang to symbolic life in two countries: the Geminian Twins were the Babylonian Mastabba.galgal, but also very probably the Two Stars of Egypt; and the Crab of Cancer was Babylonian, but also existed as the Egyptian Two Turtles, and later became the Tortoise of Greek and Chinese astrology. The symbols attached to the constellations have a long history: the Bull and Scorpion can be found, signifying spring and autumn, on a stele (commemorative stone) of Nebuchadnezzar I, who reigned during the 12th century BC.

How did the constellations get their names? Clearly, most of them were not instantly recognizable in the pictorial sense. Who could possibly claim that shown the pattern of stars which makes up, say, Taurus, they would automatically connect them into the shape of a bull? On the other hand it seems very possible that Gemini became the sign of the twins because of the bright twin stars in the constellation; Scorpio's pattern does seem to suggest a tail like that of a scorpion; and it seems similarly likely that the pattern of stars in Leo did remind someone of the silhouette of a lion.

Other connections arose for other reasons, perhaps agricultural (when the Moon was full in Virgo, for instance, the Babylonians could expect the fruition of the young standing corn), perhaps growing from the dark realms of the collective unconscious; and one or two of the signs may simply have been named as the result of some early astronomer imposing his own pattern upon a constellation for no other reason than that he needed to call it something, and the most memorable way of naming it was to connect it with a myth.

The earliest Babylonian zodiac of which we know had eighteen constellations: ten of the twelve we still use, and in addition the Pleiades, Hyades, Orion, Perseus, Auriga, Praesepe and the southern and northern fish. These are described in the mul.APIN tablets from the royal libraries of Assyria as 'constellations which stand in the path of the Moon, and into the region of which the moons pass monthly, and which they touch.'

As early as about 1000 BC a zodiac of a kind existed, even if not the one we know today. The eighteen-sign zodiac was still in use between the 6th and 3rd centuries BC. We cannot know with any certainty when the twelve-sign zodiac came into being; all we can say is that it did so very slowly and uncertainly, for even as late as the beginning of the Christian era the zodiac as we know it was not settled, although the earliest record we have of its being used for astrological prediction is from the 5th century in Babylon, and the 3rd century in Egypt.

The concept of the Great Year also arose early, and is still with us. The basic idea is that at the beginning of the world all the planets started their journeys from o degrees in Aries, and will return to that position – marking either the end of the world or the coming of the Golden Age, according to whether the astrologer is an optimist or a pessimist.

Each age is said to last for something under 26,000 years (there is of course a connection with the Precession of the Equinox); the Taurean Age is supposed to have begun in about 4139 BC, the Arian Age in about 1953 BC, the Piscean Age round about AD 220, and the Aquarian Age will begin in about 2375. These dates are of course extremely rough; no one knows when the Age of Aquarius will begin – it may already have done so, for astrologers argue that the transition from one age to another probably takes a couple of centuries.

It is perhaps interesting that as the Arian Age began, the Ram god Amun was at the height of his power in Egypt; Christianity, represented in its early years by the fish symbol so often found scratched in the Roman catacombs, began to spread throughout the world in the 2nd century AD, when the Piscean Age was beginning; and with the coming of the Aquarian Age organized religions seem to be giving way to a trust in science and world government as the twin saviours of humanity.

But what of astrology outside the Middle East? Its development in India is if anything more difficult to trace than in Babylon, for the early history of astronomy and astrology in India is not only obscure but often falsified: at least we can assume that this is so when we read the still commonly asserted statement that the first Indian astronomical textbook, the *Surya Siddhanta*, was published in the year 2,163,102 BC.

If the origins of astrology are obscure, the influences on Indian astrologers are clearer. Alexandria, for instance, had a great influence during the 6th century AD, when many Greek terms found their way into Indian astrological terminology during the lifetimes of the most famous ancient Indian astronomers, Aryabhata, Varaha Mihira and Brahmagupta. And it seems likely that the concept of the zodiac reached India via Alexandria, for Indian astrologers for some time used two sets of names for the constellations – one a straight transliteration of the Greek, the other a translation into Sanskrit; so the Greek Tauros became Taurusi, and then in Sanskrit Vrisha (the Bull), while the Greek Lēon became Leya and was then translated as Simha (the Lion).

It is strange that astrology did not make its way to India via Persia, just east of Babylonia – the gateway to Samarkand and China. But the Persian interest in the planets was quite different, in early centuries, from that of the Babylonians; its only contribution to the history of the zodiac seems to be the 'invention' of the four elements, Fire, Earth, Air and Water, later brought into the astrological scheme by Ptolemy. It was in Persia, however, that Mithraism arose – a religion that flourished between 100 BC and AD 400, and was to be responsible in large measure for the spread of astrology through the Roman empire, when as a military faith it carried belief in the influence of the planets to the furthest outposts, including Londinium. The signs of the zodiac were found in every *mithraeum*, often surrounding a carved representation of Bull sacrifice.

Neither in Persian nor in Arabic was there ever any distinction between the terms for astrology and astronomy; when the classical texts refer to *munajjimūn*, it almost always means both (and this is true throughout the world). Islamic astronomy derived from Greek, Indian and Persian sources – from Dorotheus of Sidon, Ptolemy, Antiochos of Athens, Vettius Valens and Teukros, along with Sassanid works which were often translations of Greek and Indian texts into Pahlavi, the main language of Persia in the 3rd to 7th centuries AD. Obviously Islamic astrology was a relatively late development.

The Muslims were naturally attracted to the subject, however. (The Koran seems to have encouraged them, with its various astrological references – for instance, 'He it is Who hath set for you the stars that ye may guide your course by them amid the darkness of the land and the sea.') Muslim astrologers drew up individual horoscopes and wrote astrological world histories (the best known being by Māsha'allāh and Abū Ma'shar al'Balkhī), but their chief interest was in cosmological

Astrology was only one means of divination in pre-Christian Babylonia. This clay model of a sheep's liver is inscribed with various omens and magical formulae used in attempts to foretell the future

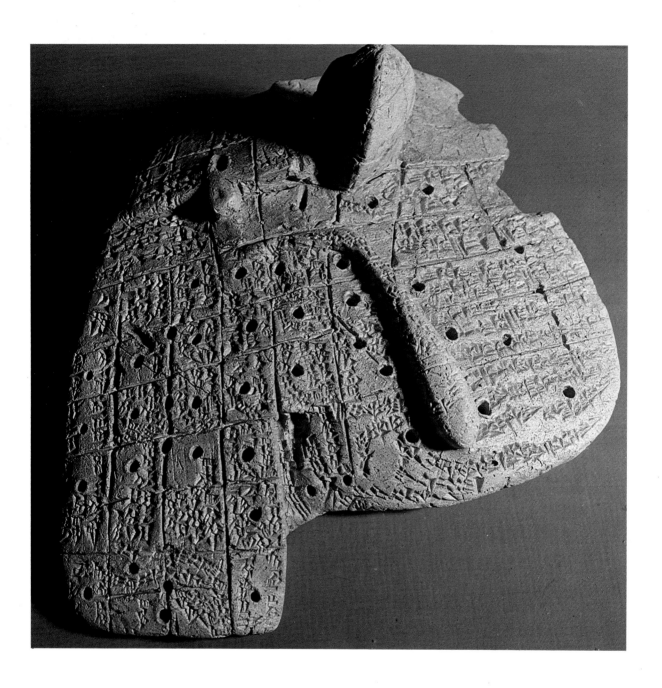

OPPOSITE **Kuddurri of Nazimaruttash, King of Babylon** *c* 1300 BC, seen here with planetary symbols and a scorpion, was like other men of his period much preoccupied with omens. He wrote asking his brother Bel-rimanni 'A cloud appeared just when I was observing the Moon. Did the eclipse take place? Please send me an exact report . . . write down your considered opinion . . .'

RIGHT **A Tang mirror** bears the Chinese 'circle of animals', only partially related to the Western zodiac. The animals seem to have been chosen by system: in April and May, tigers migrate; snakes emerge from the earth at the end of winter; pigs were put out to trample and manure the earth in August

symbolism – in astrology as it provided a means through which man could discover his own place in the cosmos and become aware of the 'reality' lying outside his own earthly life.

The Chinese have a list of twelve animals which mark their years: a child is born in the year of the boar, the rat, the ox, the tiger, the rabbit, the dragon, the snake, the horse, the sheep, the monkey, the rooster or the dog – alternatively 'positive' or 'negative' signs (the boar is 'negative'), and with the first three signs being 'water' signs, the next three 'wood', the next three 'fire' and the last three 'metal'. They are often represented in a circle (a 'zodiac' of 28 constellations was said to have originated in 2317 BC), but although there are certain very faint connections between the Western signs and the Chinese animals, these are hardly worth detailed examination. The Western zodiac was known in China by the 17th century AD, having been taken there by the Jesuits – but perhaps even earlier by travellers along the central Asian caravan routes.

The earliest Chinese astrologers did not use the ecliptic at all, but the circumpolar stars: the Chinese empire saw itself as the counterpart on

A Chinese astrologer advises a client, surrounded by the animals representing the years – that of the Cock, the Dog, the Boar, and so on. The animals can also represent the twelve double hours of the day (when they are reversed in order; the annual circle is counted anti-clockwise, the daily circle clockwise)

earth of the Middle Kingdom of Heaven, the region of the stars that never set – the circumpolar stars are indeed seen all year round. The Emperor, representing the Pole Star, sat facing south to give audience; and his astrologers used an obscure system of four 'Palaces'. It was only in the 1st century AD that the ecliptic was given a name in Chinese: 'The Yellow Road', as opposed to the equator, which was 'The Red Road'.

It has sometimes been supposed that astrology did not reach the Americas until at least the age of Columbus. Historians assume that when the Bishop of Chiapas wrote in 1698 that certain sections of the Quiché, an ancient Peruvian tribe, 'believe that the birth of man is regulated by the course of the stars and planets; they observe the time of the day and the month at which a child is born, and predict the conditions of its life and destiny', he was reporting the use of astrological techniques brought to South America by the Spaniards. But there was certainly a kind of astrology in use in Mexico before Columbus, even if it was based on a system unlike anything in Europe: Toltec astronomy, for instance, divided the world into five 'directions' – north, south, east, west and centre, the first four ruled by the Bull, Lion, Eagle and Man. (These coincide somewhat with the European fixed signs of the zodiac, Taurus, Leo, Scorpio and Aquarius, much later associated with the symbols of the four Apostles – Luke (the Bull), Mark (the Lion), John (the Eagle) and Matthew (the Man, or Aquarius).

The mystery of how the constellations used in the zodiac acquired their own characteristics – why astrologers should have begun to associate Gemini with liveliness and versatility, Aries with courage and selfishness, Libra with charm and ease – is unfathomable. The association made by early man between the planets and certain human characteristics is easier to understand: the Sun, blazing in all its glory, was certainly the major visible symbol of royalty and nobility, pompous and domineering; equally, the Moon's association with motherhood can safely be associated with its influence on the female cycle, and on the feminine element, water – the rivers and seas with their regular tides. One may even suggest that Mars was associated with aggression because of its relatively fiery, red appearance in the bright night skies, and Venus with beauty and love because of its clear, bright steadiness. On the other hand, how did Jupiter come to be associated with optimism and justice, Saturn with practicality and caution?

These characteristics appeared very early. In 235 BC, an astrologer told a client that 'If your child is born when Venus comes forth and Jupiter has set, his wife will be stronger than he' – Venus associated with indecision and laziness, Jupiter with kindliness, loyalty, ease. The same astrologer associated Leo with wealth and power, Cancer with water, Taurus with strength in battle. To all these simple associations modern astrologers would to some extent assent.

Astrologers argue that associations between the signs and planets and certain characteristics were empirically made: that over the centuries it became clear that man was more amorous when Venus was prominent, more prone to violence when Mars was active; that when certain planets were in Gemini at the time of the birth of a baby, it would grow up to be talkative, quick-moving and hasty. And certainly there is much evidence to suggest that the elaboration of the techniques of astrology came about not through psychic guesswork, or even the symbolic unconscious, but (as in science) through observation and careful record.

However that may be, once the signs and planets had begun to assume their characteristics, the zodiac was formed and a reliable calendar devised, the last ingredient was available for the development of the horoscope as we know it, and of modern astrology. The simple omens of early times were about to give way to more elaborate predictions: at first still relatively simple, but becoming more and more complex until far from such simple statements as 'If a child is born when the Moon is come forth, his life will be bright, excellent, regular and long', astrologers would be able to write many thousands of words about the personality, character, potential, health and motivations of a new-born child.

II

THE PRESTIGIOUS PLANETS

THE planets, seen as gods, played so early a part in prophesy and divination that evidence of their effect on the history of Babylonia is hard to come by. Even when it does present itself, it is extremely uncertain when concerned with dates earlier than about the 10th century BC.

Copies of copies of documents from the library of Sargon of Agade, who ruled Babylonia in about 2000 BC, suggest that he instructed his astrologers to choose propitious moments for starting ambitious projects, and his library no doubt contained collections of star omens. But it is only with the mul.APIN, three thousand years later, which summarizes the astronomical knowledge of its time, that we approach the realm of fact rather than conjecture; here are accounts of genuine observations of the movements of the planets as they travelled three Roads - the Road of Anu, god of the northern sky, of Enlil, god of the atmosphere (the path which the Greeks christened the ecliptic, and later the zodiac), and of Ea, god of the deep. The laborious gathering of the facts enshrined in these tablets must have gone on for centuries: there are hints of a set of tablets dating from the time of Hammurapi, sixteen hundred years earlier, which record the movements of Venus - even then perhaps used in connection with the interpretation of certain omens.

It was in the 7th century BC that the earliest astrologers of whom we know were recorded, during the reigns of Esarhaddon (681-668) and his successor Assurbanipal. Esarhaddon employed Akkullanu, Balasi, Ishtar-shumeresh, Nabun-adinshum and Nabua-heriba; Assurbanipal's

Assurbanipal, who became king of Assyria in 669 BC, was, like all heads of state, much concerned to preserve and extend means of divination. He brought from Calah to Nineveh the great astronomical library of Nabu, helping to amalgamate the available knowledge of Babylon and Egyptian astronomer-astrologers. A great antiquarian, he also preserved in fifteen tablets the records of the astrological rituals of the months astrological advisers included Adad-shumusur, Mar-Ishtar and Belu-shezib. The astrologers were established in workshops or studios attached to the temple of Ea, the god of oracles and inventor of writing. At the outset of his reign Esarhaddon instructed them to calculate for him the best time at which he should start restoring the images of the gods and rebuilding their sanctuaries. He also asked more personal questions: was it a good time for his son to visit him? (his predecessor had been murdered by his offspring); would he find the coming eclipse dangerous? These simple questions are among the first personal enquiries on record.

The weight that Esarhaddon gave to his astrologers' interpretations of the movements of the planets sprang from his reverence for the planets themselves. The preamble of his important treaty with a Median king begins:

In the presence of the planets Jupiter, Venus, Saturn, Mercury, Mars, Sirius, and in the presence of Assur, Anu, Enlil, Ea, Sin, Shamash ...

Thus the planet-gods are given precedence over the ancient territorial gods – even before Shamash the Sun and Sin the Moon.

Naturally, such prestigious personalities as these gods of the skies must control the most important matters within their dominions. Diodorus says that the Babylonians called the five planets the Interpreters because they decided the fate of both individuals and nations. The planetary forecasts that have survived naturally concern kings and governors, but it was accepted that at least one planet-god held sway over the birth of even the lowliest individual – and Diodorus reports that the Babylonians took into consideration the influences of twenty-four stars known as 'the judges of the world', and thirty stars called 'consulting gods'. Which stars these were, and whether there were fifty-four separate ones or the same star sometimes shared a dual function, we do not know.

It is doubtful whether the people of Babylonia – even, it may be, the rulers – knew much about the intricacies of the astrology practised by their astrologer-priests. They got a glimpse of astrological lore through the myths and legends of their civilization: most notably in *The Epic of Gilgamesh*, the ruler of Sumer, surviving fragmentarily on twelve tablets from the library of Assurbanipal at Nineveh. Each of his twelve adventures relates to a sign of the zodiac: he meets a Scorpion Man in the sign of Scorpio, reaches the Waters of Death in Capricorn, consults a half-man, half-bull called Ea-bani in Taurus, and receives a proposal of marriage from the goddess Ishtar in Virgo. The Babylonians, on hearing these stories, learned to regard their own lives too as a quest for immortality, running parallel to that of the Sun god as he travelled through the constellations.

The earliest individual predictions were made without the help of the zodiac, and when they were made for a king were interpreted as applying to the whole kingdom: an unfortunate month for the monarch meant an unfortunate month for the state. Even so, some crude personal predictions have survived for non-royal individuals. There is a Babylonian omen text from the second half of the second millenium which predicts certain events from the month of a child's birth – crude indeed; as crude as the modern astrological paperbacks that tell you what your child will be like if he or she is born 'under' a certain sign.

The earliest surviving horoscope, now in the Bodleian Library at Oxford, is dated 410 BC, and is for the son of Shuma-usar, son of Shuma-iddina, descendant of Deke, who was born when 'the Moon was below the Horn of the Scorpion, Jupiter in the Fish, Venus in the Bull, Saturn in the Crab, Mars in the Twins. Mercury, which had set ... was ... invisible.' There is no interpretation given for this child; a modern astrologer would say that he was sensual and loving, possessive and jealous, with powerful instincts and emotions, had a strong sense of patriarchal tradition, was financially shrewd and ambitious, prone to periods of restlessness and possibly incapable of consistent steady work. A later horoscope, for 4 April 253 BC, though much damaged, did offer an interpretation: 'He will be lacking in wealth ... His food will not suffice for his hunger. The wealth he had in his youth will not stay. His days will be long. His wife, whom people will seduce in his presence, will ...' And there, alas, the story breaks off.

It should be pointed out that these earliest horoscopes were not set out within the familiar circle of a 'modern' horoscope, representing a map of the sky for a particular moment and place, nor in the earlier square form which persisted until the 17th century, and is sometimes seen even today. They were merely lists of the positions of the planets.

The word horoscope, incidentally, derives from the Greek *hōroskópos*, meaning the sign ascending over the eastern horizon at a given moment (from *hōra*, time, and *skopós*, observer).

By the 3rd century BC astrologers had at their command a proper almanac giving the positions of the Moon and planets at regular intervals over a number of years, together with conjunctions of the Sun and Moon. These suggested an order in an otherwise orderless, incoherent universe, an order man should strive to emulate; the movements of planets in the skies had meaning which man was capable of understanding, and related to his life – otherwise why should the planets move at all? It could not be that they were the products of accident. This theory had great political importance, and is advanced again and again over the next two thousand years throughout Europe, as an argument in favour of order in society.

The idea that the influence of the planets was all-pervading, and that a true interpreter of that influence was of enormous value, was widely spread in the centuries just before the death of Christ, by the Chaldeans. The term should really always be written in inverted commas. Chaldea was properly a province of Babylonia, whose citizens soon became the élite of the country, virtually dominating its ruling class as early as the 8th century BC. Eventually, 'Babylonia' and 'Chaldea' became interchangeable terms; but for some reason the popular meaning of the term 'Chaldean' came to be 'astrologer'. In the Book of Daniel, for instance, 'Chaldean' always meant that – or mathematician, astronomer, wizard or magician!

Many leading astrologers were literally Chaldeans, although many no doubt came from other areas of Babylonia or other parts of the Middle East. Even countries not noted for a special interest in astrology had a contribution to make. Persia, for instance, produced El Hakim, otherwise Gjamasp, a court astrologer to the semi-legendary king Hystaspes of Iran in the 6th century BC, who wrote a book in which he examined the effect of the conjunctions of Jupiter and Saturn on the history of the world. *Judicia Gjamaspis* offered predictions that have been interpreted as foreseeing the birth of Christ and the rise of Islam.

In India, certain predictions were already possible by the 6th century BC, as we see from the works of Varaha Mihira, whose astronomical textbook, the *Brihat Samhita*, suggests that the portents to be seen in the skies are so many and so complex that every astrologer should have at least four assistants, and that 'the king who does not honour a scholar accomplished in horoscopy and astronomy, clever in all branches and accessories, comes to grief.'

But it was the Chaldeans, predominantly, who carried astrology to other nations and broadened its scope, claiming for the first time for instance that not only a man, but a city, could have its 'moment of birth', and that therefore an astrologer could advise on the laying of the foundation stone at an auspicious moment, in order to give the city a horoscope encouraging security and prosperity. One of the first instances we find of an astrologer offering advice on that subject is in about 312 BC, when Seleucus I founded the city of Seleucia on the Tigris. Seleucus was a devout adherent of astrology (unlike his chief antagonist Antigonos, who ignored the prediction that Seleucus would kill him on the field of battle, which he did, in 301). When he was planning Seleucia he

A Babylonian horoscope, written on papyrus, and dated 1 April AD 81. There was much concern with 'lucky' and 'unlucky' days (sometimes a day would be divided into three parts, each part marked as 'lucky' or 'unlucky'); but there were often more particular predictions: 'Do not go forth from your house from any side of it [today], and hold no intercourse with women … Whoever is born on this day will die of excessive love-making'; or, four days later, 'whoever is born on this day will die of old age'

consulted a number of Chaldeans. These were, like the Babylonians, against the idea of the new city, which they suspected (rightly) would in time mean the desertion and ruin of Babylon itself. They therefore worked out the *least* auspicious time for the cornerstone of the new city to be laid, and advised Seleucus accordingly. He issued his orders; but his workmen were so eager to raise the city that they started work before the given time, thus providing the city with a highly propitious horoscope!

The birth chart of Seleucia is lost. That for another of Seleucus' cities, Antioch, has survived – calculated for 22 May 300 BC – as have those for Constantinople, Alexandria, Gaza, Caesarea; sometimes representations of parts of these were engraved on coins minted in the cities concerned.

From Babylonia, the Chaldeans carried astrology into Egypt, and more importantly into Greece. The enormous importance in Egypt of myths about the sky gods, the travels and adventures of Sin, the Moon god, Shamash the Sun god, or Ishtar the personification of Venus, have led people to believe that that country must have made a great contribution to the development of astrology. In fact, its interest in the planets came fairly late – apart from a devotion to Venus, which anyway was seen as a star of the morning and evening rather than as a planet.

The impression that the Egyptians had a long tradition of astrological knowledge probably arose because they were jealous of the older tradition of Babylonia. When in 260 BC Berosus (supported by Diodorus and Cicero) claimed that the Chaldean astrological texts were almost half a million years old, Egyptian astronomers countered by claiming that their texts dated from at least 630,000 BC.

Just as with the other advanced civilizations, there was certainly an early interest in astronomical events. Egyptian texts dating from as early as the 13th century BC show a familiarity with the positions of the stars; but the Egyptian obsession was more with the devising of a workable calendar than with any astrological significance. They turned to other omens for prediction: the cry of a new-born child, for instance, or its appearance. If it turned its eyes towards the Sun, it was a sign of early death. They interpreted dreams, too, and employed necromancy.

Discussion about the place of the pyramids in the development of astrology in Egypt seems fruitless. It is no doubt the case that some if not all of the pyramids were constructed for astronomical purposes, or at the very least with astronomy in mind; and since astronomy was indistinguishable from astrology, there is no point in denying that for instance the Great Pyramid, built in about 2500 BC, has a place in astrological history. But what place?

Innumerable theories have been advanced to explain the pyramids and to discover their secrets. As early as 1883 it was suggested that they had been erected as astronomical observatories and star clocks. Years later, it was proposed that the Egyptians who built the Great Pyramid must have known that the earth was round, and flattened at the poles, that they could measure the precise length of the year and had mastered a system of map projection.

The claim that the first horoscope was cast in Egypt in 2767 BC is suspect, although there is certainly a diagram of that date representing a particular moment of time – not, as far as we know, connected with the birth or life of a particular individual, but an early affirmation of belief that a particular moment of time had an individual significance (a proposition echoed in the 20th century by the psychologist C. G. Jung). Its existence shows that the early Egyptians were capable of close observation of the heavens; they may have used the pyramids for that purpose.

When the tomb of Rameses II was excavated, it was found to contain two circles of gold marked in 360 degrees, and with symbols showing the rising and setting of stars. This suggests that he was interested in ascending degrees – the degree of the ecliptic rising over the eastern horizon at any particular time, an important matter in astrology. Rameses II –

A coffin from Thebes (of the 2nd century AD) shows the Egyptian goddess Nut surrounded by the signs of the Zodiac. Nut, the sky goddess, represented the vault of heaven

Ozymandias, the builder of the temple at Abu Simbel – reigned from about 1292–1225 BC; and the tomb of Rameses V contained papyri offering astrological hints for every hour of every month of the year.

There is evidence too that astrologers in the Egypt of thirteen hundred years before Christ knew about the four fixed signs of the zodiac (astrologers divide the signs into *quadruplicities* or *qualities* – cardinal, mutable, and fixed). In the sarcophagus of Seti I (*c* 1317 BC) the four jars containing the intestines were protected by four deities, represented with a human head (Mestha), a dog's head (Hapi), a jackal's head (Tuamutef) and a hawk's head (Qebhsennuf). These clearly represented the four fixed signs, with Mestha as Aquarius, Hapi as Leo, Tuamutef as Taurus and Qebhsennuf as Scorpio. But this is not a sign that advanced astrology was

One of two horoscopes on the ceiling of a tomb at Athribis, and dated 14 February AD 177

practised: the four Suns of Horus were the gods of astronomical myths, with astrological associations.

A major contribution to the early history of astrology was, however, made by Egypt: the invention of the decans by the division of the circle of the ecliptic into thirty-six sections, three decans or sections of 10 degrees to each sign. The earliest sight we have of these is on a coffin lid of the Middle Kingdom, on which the sky is shown with the names of the decans in columns. The zodiac did not then exist: the decans were geared to the constellations, and it was not until the Hellenistic age that they were linked with the zodiac and became truly astrological in significance. It seems that they were contrived because of the Egyptian belief that every moment of time should have its presiding deity.

Stobaeus, who collected valuable extracts from Greek authors in the 5th century AD, in an essay addressed to his son, claimed that the decans exert their influence on bodies from on high. How could they not act on us as well, on each in particular and on all men together? Thus, my child, among all the catastrophes of universal scope due to forces emanating from them, we may cite as examples – mark well my words – the changes of kings, the uprisings of cities, famines, pestilences, flux and reflux of the sea, earthquakes. Nothing of all that, my child, occurs without the influence of the decans.

The circular zodiac found by Napoleon on the ceiling of the temple of Hat-Hor, goddess of heaven, at Denderah, in Egypt, in 1798, and now in the Louvre museum. It was originally thought to be immeasurably ancient, but in fact the temple itself was only built during the reign of the Roman emperor Tiberius, and the zodiac has been dated 16 April AD 17

The decans were later to be specially important in medical astrology, when different ailments were specific to different decans (stomach trouble, for instance, being attributable to the first decanate of Virgo).

Despite their interest in star patterns, Egyptian astrologers were not nearly as advanced as their Babylonian colleagues. Their mathematics were even more cumbrous and the zodiac reached them comparatively late – the earliest of which we have a report was engraved on the ceiling of a hall north of Esna some time before 221 BC. There are only slight differences between the earliest surviving Egyptian zodiacs (at Esna and in the chapel of Osiris at Denderah, built at about the time of Christ) and those of Babylonia; clearly the zodiac came to Egypt directly from there.

And what use was made of astrology in Egypt? There were certainly predictions for the Pharaoh and for the country: 'the Flood will come to Egypt'; 'many men will rebel against the King'; 'seed and grain will be high in price'; 'the burial of a god will occupy Egypt.' All these predictions were made on the basis of movements of the Dog star, Sothis – 'If Sothis rises when the Moon is in the Archer', or 'If Sothis rises when Mercury is in the Twins', and so on.

Another papyrus, from the Roman period, makes predictions for individuals based on the presence of Venus and Mercury in the 'houses' of the horoscope at the time of birth. (The 'houses' are twelve divisions within the circle of the horoscope, relating to particular areas of life. The system was invented by the Babylonians and persists even now, although astrologers have disagreed about the system of house division.)

Astrology had a part to play in formal religion, and sometimes a major one. Clement of Alexandria, a distinguished Christian writer born in about AD 150, describes an Egyptian religious procession of his own time, but with traditional and ancient elements:

First goes the Precentor carrying two of Hermes' books, one containing the Hymns of the Gods, the other directions for the kingly office. After him follows the Horoscopus, an expert in the four astrological books of Hermes. Then succeeds the Hierogrammateus, or sacred scribe, with feathers upon his head, and a book and rule in his hands, to whom it belongeth to be thoroughly acquainted with the hieroglyphics, as with cosmography, geography, the order of the Sun and Moon and five planets ...

'The four astrological books of Hermes' came from that legendary collection of ancient texts the Hermetic books. These were allegedly collected together by the Egyptian god Thoth, later known to the Greeks as Hermes Trismegistus, and still later to the Romans as Mercury. Some authorities believed that there were forty-two volumes of these texts; other historians were more adventurous – Seleucus claimed that there were twenty thousand volumes, and Manethon was particular, having counted 36,525.

The texts, however many there were, enshrined traditional knowledge about religion, art, science, geometry, alchemy, astronomy, astrology and many other subjects. They were held to be sacred, and only the highest of Egyptian priests were allowed to touch them. Alas, no one has yet discovered the tomb of Alexander the Great, in which the Emperor Severus is supposed to have entombed the last complete set. It may be that the extreme veneration in which the texts were held was a major factor in their not surviving; they were so sacred that only a few people were permitted access to them, and perhaps there came a time when those few had all died without ensuring that their charge had been passed on to posterity. However, the absence of any real knowledge of the texts has not prevented an enormous literature growing up about them, and it has never been doubted that any large collection of traditional wisdom, however put together, would certainly have contained much ancient theory about astrology.

Hermes was supposed to have devised an astrological system of his own, and among the Hermetic books was, apparently, one on medical astrology, another on the decans (including a detailed catalogue going back beyond 150 BC), one on zodiacal plants, and one on the astrological degrees. Hermes' writings are quoted freely by many later astrologers, including Thrasyllus, perhaps the most influential of all astrologers of Imperial Rome, Antiochus of Athens, and Sarapion, a pupil of Hipparchus, the Greek astronomer.

To what extent pieces of the original texts have survived – and obviously there *were* original texts, whether or not they were written by Hermes – it is difficult to say; large claims have been made (and not only by the ancients, at that). Some fragments of very early astrological texts have come down to us, via the Greeks. In the 5th century AD, a Latin text, *Liber Hermetis*, translated from the Greek, gives a muddled mixture of theory about the decans, conjunctions, the meanings of certain planets in certain signs, and advice on personal matters – how to predict the day of death, useful or difficult days, marriage, duration of life – which seems to derive from a very early original. It pays special attention to the decans: the third decan of Gemini is responsible for muscular pains, the first of Virgo controls the stomach, the first of Cancer the heart, and so on. It is in this text that the Astrological Man makes his first appearance: onto a figure of the body is imposed the zodiac circle, straightened out – the first sign, Aries, at the head, and the last, Pisces, at the feet. Between them various parts of the body fall under the influence of the signs in their order. It is a system still used today, although with some amendments: Libra for instance is now said to 'rule' the kidneys, whereas Hermes claimed it affected the buttocks.

A passage from the *Liber Hermetis* will do very well to summarize the general attitude to astrology as it was when the Chaldeans had passed it on to the Greeks as a systemized whole:

Man is called by the informed, a World, since he is wholly correspondent with the World's nature. Indeed at the moment of conception there spurts from the seven planets a whole complex of rays that bear on each part of the man.

And the same thing happens at the birth-hour, according to the position of the twelve signs. Thus the Ram is called the head, and the head's sense-organs are shared out among the seven planets. The right eye goes to the Sun, the left to the Moon, and ears to Saturn, the brain to Jupiter, the tongue and uvula to Mercury, smelling and taste to Venus, all the blood-vessels to Mars.

If then at the moment of conception or birth one of the stars finds itself in a bad condition, there is produced an infirmity in the member corresponding with that star. For instance, a man has four main parts: head, thorax, hands, feet. One of these has become infirm at the conception-moment or at birth somewhere by its heavenly patron having been itself in a bad way; an eye, the two eyes, an ear, the two ears, or again the teeth have undergone some damage or speech has been blurred; the ray of a malevolent planet has come to strike one of those parts, spoil and corrupt it.

It is interesting that the anonymous writer or writers apparently believed that the planets' position should be observed not only at the moment of birth of a child but at the moment of conception. Throughout the history of astrology there have been arguments about this. The moment of birth is obviously the more convenient to record – indeed, it is normally impossible to know the precise moment of conception, although if personal astrology works because of the overt influence of the planets on the forming embryo, the moment of conception must surely be nearer the time when the influence is exerted than the moment of birth. But the presentation of man as microcosm and the world, or even the universe, as macrocosm, is one to which almost every astrologer since AD 400 has subscribed.

The Hermetic texts, in as far as we can guess at their total content, presented astrology to the Western world not only as a method of divination but as a religious conception of the world and man's place in it. It was to be inseparably combined with Greek philosophy, and to be increasingly important not only to philosophers and rulers but to the man in the street.

OPPOSITE ABOVE On the ceiling of the tomb of Seti I (*c* 1300 BC) a Bull represents the Great Bear. Elsewhere the seven stars are seen grouped in the pattern of the Bull's Foreleg; both Bull and foreleg are connected with Horus, the ferryman, much associated with the planets: 'He ascends to heaven among the imperishable stars …'

OPPOSITE BELOW In the tomb of Rameses VI of Egypt drawings show how far the Egyptians progressed in their attempts at astronomical observation; stars are shown against a grid of lines, and some of them named (occasionally wrongly, for the craftsman who made the drawing did not always understand what he was being asked to do)

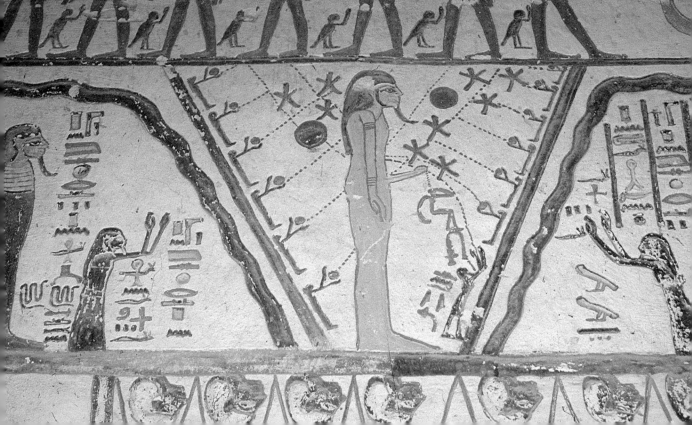

euoln
ao Ante
Anm eft
a caufa
tis cur
fus folis
Ab vno m̃
ueo in ꝗ
libet gra
dus flanu
uis sigñ
vsꝗ̃ Ad
eub̃ red
ditum̃ ad
idem pūc
tũ licet
posset ali
ter forte

diffinire ꝓut nimbus dam̃ visum eft. Et illud con
siderátur secundũ duos modos vel secundũ ze
nolucionem̃ divuem̃ natum̃ tatinꝰ ꝭuꝭ obicti

III

THROUGH THE DOORS OF GREECE

ALEXANDER the Great was born, history tells us, the son of King Philip II of Macedon. Legend has it, however, that the boy's real father was a King of Egypt, Nectanebus, among whose accomplishments was the art of summoning immense armies out of thin air. In 356 BC, the planets informed him that his enemies would triumph over him, however efficient his aerial forces, so he packed his bags and made off, heavily disguised, to Macedon, where he set up as an astrologer and ingratiated himself at court. While the king was away, Nectanebus, with the aid of wax dolls and other magical means, transported himself into the queen's bedroom disguised as the god Ammon, to whose blandishments Olympias naturally felt bound to accede. She became pregnant.

When her term came, Nectanebus came to her room and set up at her bedside a tablet made of gold, silver and acacia wood, which stood on a tripod and consisted of three belts - one with Zeus on it, surrounded by the thirty-six decans; then one bearing the twelve signs of the zodiac; and on the innermost the Sun and Moon. To these he fitted eight precious stones showing the positions of the planets. He begged her not to give birth until these were propitious - and when they were, with a flash of lightning and a thump of thunder, Alexander was born. We are not told of King Philip's reaction on returning to discover the *fait accompli*; and indeed other accounts suggest that he and the queen merely employed an astrologer to tell the new-born child's fortune. But of Alexander's later successes, history tells us at length.

OPPOSITE A scribe presents an edition of a work by Ptolemy to King Henry VI of England. The *Tetrabiblos*, which correlated the astrological knowledge available in Ptolemy's time (the first half of the 2nd century AD) was used as a textbook by astrologers for well over a thousand years

Nectanebus is said to have become Alexander's tutor, using as text-book *The Secret of Secrets*, a book by Aristotle, later lost. This, among other things, circulated a knowledge of and respect for astrology. It did Nectanebus no good, however, for when the child was 12 years old he tipped the astrologer over a cliff to prove that he could not foretell the time of his own death. But at least it apparently provided many useful tips for the future world general – such as that he should never take a laxative except when the Moon was in Scorpio, Libra or Pisces, and that severe constipation would result were he to be unwise enough to take one while the Moon was in Capricorn.

It has always been understood that Alexander made use of astrology throughout his campaigns, though whether because he believed in it, or knew that others believed, and took advantage of the fact, is far from clear. It seems unlikely that he almost alone among educated people of his time placed the influence of the planets at naught – although one or two philosophers did so: Eudoxus (*c* 408–355 BC), for instance, the inventor of the geometrical theory of proportion, who demanded that 'no credence should be given to the Chaldeans, who predict and mark out the life of every man according to the day of his nativity'. And the Greek Academy under Carneades and Clitomachus, in the 1st century BC, was to set itself firmly against divination, magic and astrology.

But they were in a tiny minority. In general, as the historian Gilbert Murray was to put it, 'astrology fell upon the Hellenistic mind as a new disease falls upon some remote island people'. Through such outposts as Daphnae, a Greek settlement in Egypt between 610 and 560 BC, and especially through the ports of Egypt opened to Greek ships after 640 BC, travelling Chaldean astrologers descended on Greece in considerable numbers, bringing with them the apparently age-old wisdom they had hoarded, which was received warmly by Greeks already better practised in mathematics and astronomy than they.

If any evidence was needed of the fact that much astronomical and astrological lore came directly from Babylonia to Greece, we have only to look at the names of the planets. When the Greeks first recognized these, they called them Herald of the Dawn (Venus, noted even by Homer for its brightness, although sometimes it was called Vespertine, as the star of the evening), the Twinkling Star (Mercury), the Fiery Star (Mars), the Luminous Star (Jupiter), and the Brilliant Star (Saturn). But after the 4th century, these names begin to disappear, and others to take their place – Aphrodite, Hermes, Ares, Zeus and Cronos.

It seems almost certain that the reason is that by then the Chaldeans had arrived with their barbaric names for the planets – Nebo, Ishtar,

Nergal, Marduk and Ninib. The Greeks simply substituted their own deities' names for the foreign ones – so today we call the planets by names that are English renderings of Latin translations of Greek translations of the original Babylonian ones!

One of the reasons for astrology's success in the Greek world may well have been the atmosphere during the period after Alexander's death, when the ancient ideal of the Greek republic was being replaced by the concept of universal monarchy. Religion was in a sense internationalized, and the worship of the planets and stars as deities became stronger as the cities lost their individual powers and personalities. The planets spread their influences indiscriminately, and such philosophers as Zeno, the founder of Stoicism, believing that nothing was determined by chance (indeed, that there was no such thing as chance) emphasized in the 4th century BC the idea that earthly happenings were rigidly determined by natural laws. What then was more obvious than that the planets, coolly moving in their predetermined courses, were the governors of events?

There is also, of course, the Greek expertise at astronomy and mathematics, and ingenuity in constructing machines to match that expertise: Ptolemy describes the construction of an astrolabe, an instrument for measuring the positions of the stars; and a little machine with geared wheels, discovered in the sunken wreck of a vessel of the 1st century BC, seems to have been devised to work out the motions of the planets. If some Greek ideas about the constitution of the solar system were distinctly eccentric (Ptolemy's not least so) their grasp of mechanics and mathematics was brilliant – much more so than many historians of the 18th century believed.

If we can safely ignore Philostratus' claim (made in the 3rd century AD) that astrology was known and practised in Greece as early as 1184 BC, it is certainly the case that Hesiod, a poet who lived in the 8th century BC, paid attention to the positions of the planets and stars in his *Works and Days*. In this long poem he suggested among other things that they should be used to predict good times at which to start certain tasks.

The Greeks pioneered enormous developments in astronomical theory. Aristotle disproved Anaximander's theory that the Earth floats freely and without support; Pythagoras was probably the first man to 'know' (if without proof) that the world was one of the planets, and round. This theory, first put forward it seems by Philolaus of Thebes at the end of the 5th century BC, was based on intuition rather than on reason, but the guess was an important one. It was clear by this time, too – at least to some astronomers – that the Sun was much larger than the Earth, and therefore probably the latter was not the centre of the universe. And by

230 BC, Aristarchus of Samos, centuries before Copernicus, argued that the Earth and all the planets revolved in circles round the Sun, the Earth turning on its axis once in twenty-four hours. But the time was against him, and only his colleague Seleucus accepted his theory, which otherwise sank like a stone – although Copernicus was heartened, pursuing it in his own age, to find evidence of an ancient conviction of the hypothesis.

The Greeks seem to have adopted the zodiac as early as the 6th century BC; it may have been Democritus, round about 420, who popularized it and the idea that the planets influenced man as they travelled through the signs. It is said that he spent much time in Egypt and the east; certainly he visited Persia, and he may have been more decided in advancing his view that the planets governed men's lives than any Greek before him. He agreed with Zeno that nothing could happen in the world by chance. It has been claimed that he gave the zodiac signs their Greek names, although other historians have suggested that Anaxagoras, born in Ionia in about 500 BC, may have had a hand in that – he was an adventurous astronomer, the first to explain that the Moon shone because of the reflected light of the Sun. He was thrown out of Athens, where he lived for thirty years, for attempting to rationalize astronomy, and teaching rationalist theories about 'the things on high'. The Greeks, who sacrificed to the Sun and Moon, were outraged at his suggestion that they were paying court to a 'fiery star' and a lump of earth.

Many reports of early astronomical/astrological feats by the Greeks must be regarded with suspicion. It has often been suggested, for instance, that Thales predicted a solar eclipse that occurred in 585 BC, thus ending a battle between the Lydians and Medes, who stopped fighting in sheer surprise. This seems unlikely. The knowledge simply did not exist by which it could have been done, although it is possible Thales might simply have made a spectacularly successful guess. There is a little more substance, perhaps, in Pliny's report that Cleostratus of Tenedos observed the zodiacal constellations as they appeared behind Mount Ida towards the end of the 6th century. But it is only on looking at the calendars devised by Eudoxos of Cnidus (c 408–355 BC), a Greek scientist and astronomer, that we definitely find use being made of the Greek zodiac (it was he who, in the *Phainomena*, divided the ecliptic into twelve equal signs).

Between the 5th century BC and the birth of Christ, astrology appealed to various sections of Greek society, among them not only philosophers and scientists, but such men as Hippocrates, the physician and 'father of medicine', who taught astrology to his students so that they could discover the 'critical days' in an illness. He is said to have remarked that 'any man who does not understand astrology is a fool rather than a physician'. And the young intelligentsia often took an intense interest in the subject; when Plato visited Dionysus' school, he saw two pupils arguing with great vigour about the theories of Anaxagoras, illustrating their argument by imitating the sweep of the ecliptic with their arms. Aristophanes in *The Clouds* ridicules the study of astrology as one of the cults of the Athens upper classes.

It was, as might be expected, a Chaldean - Berosus, a priest of Bel Marduk at Babylon - who in about 260 BC came to the island of Cos, where there was a medical school at which Hipparchus had taught, and set up there a formal school of astrology which was perhaps the earliest such establishment. He seems to have used for his textbook a treatise called *The Eye of Bel*, which existed in the form of seventy tablets in the library of Assurbanipal, but was compiled much earlier, in the 3rd millenium BC, for Sargon I - or so it was said. Berosus also wrote an enormous history of his homeland, *Babylonica*, covering some five hundred thousand years from the creation of the world to the death of Alexander the Great, setting out in it a considerable amount of astronomical/astrological lore: about the Great Year, for instance, and the theory that earthquakes were caused by planets being in conjunction with the Sun. He also predicted a cataclysmic world disaster when all the planets were in conjunction in Cancer: the earth would become mud during an inordinate flood, and the world would eventually be covered with water, sweeping away all human life.

Berosus was famous in his own time, and it is said that Athens raised a statue of him with a golden tongue, to pay tribute to his oratorical skills. He was succeeded on Cos by Antipatrus and Achinapolus, who taught medical astrology, and seem to have been the first non-Babylonian astrologers to experiment with the idea of drawing up a horoscope for the moment of conception rather than birth. They worked a good deal on the ancient aphorism, preserved in Hermetic literature, to the effect that the sign occupied by the Moon at the moment of conception would be in the ascendant at the time of birth. Interestingly Dr Eugen Jonas, a Czechoslovak psychiatrist, did a great deal of work on the same theory in the 1960s, claiming to be able to predict by the tropical position of the Moon at the time of conception the sex of a child, before birth. The Communist government banned his work in 1970, before his full evidence could be published.

Dimly, we hear of other visiting Chaldean travellers to Greece: Soudines, for instance, a visitor to the court of Attalus I, King of Pergamum, who compiled lunar tables which were used for centuries, and one of the earliest lapidaries, associating various precious stones with certain planets and signs. By now, many Greeks were quick to adopt the new celestial theory: Epigenes of Byzantium, Apollonius of Myndus and Artemidorus of Parium all boasted of having been instructed by Babylonian priest-astrologers. Kidenas, who probably lived in the second half of the 3rd century BC, seems to have been responsible for some Babylonian astronomical discoveries, and perhaps was a tutor of Berosus himself (though one of the problems is that the dates of many of these early astrologers are extremely uncertain). Then there was Aratus, a contemporary of Berosus, who in about 276 BC versified the *Phainomena* of Eudoxos, producing a poem which became required reading for generations of Greeks, with its account of the planets, the zodiac and the other constellations, and its concluding advice to meteorologists:

> Study the Signs together through the year,
> Then never of the weather shall a guess
> Make random nonsense, but assured forecast.

Innumerable Greek and Roman commentators published their own editions of Aratus.

A misty figure with the name Critodemus appears briefly in a list of the founders of the Greek astrological tradition given by Firmicus Maternus, a Latin writer of about AD 356, in his *De erroribus profanorum religionum*, among purely imaginary personages such as Hermes, Orpheus and Nechepso. This kind of thing plagues anyone attempting to trace astrological history. Was Critodemus imaginary too? Or did he indeed construct the horoscopes he is said to have drawn up? There is a treatise ascribed to him, *Horasis*, from which later astrologers learned: one, Hephaistion, relied utterly on his astrological formula for determining whether a child would be still-born.

Gradually, astrological lore was being drawn together into a more or less coherent body of knowledge. This did not mean, however, that it was free of contradictions, or that it developed with any more coherence than other theories about the nature of the universe. In the three centuries before the birth of Christ, splits occurred between astrologers which continue to this day. Perhaps the chief one concerned free will. One school of 'scientific' astrologers took a severely empirical view: everything was predetermined, and the movements of the planets were, so to speak, geared to coming events. Another, the 'catharchic' school, believed that some things were predetermined, but by no means all. If you studied the planets' movements sufficiently minutely, you could by seizing a propitious moment bring about success when to act at another moment might

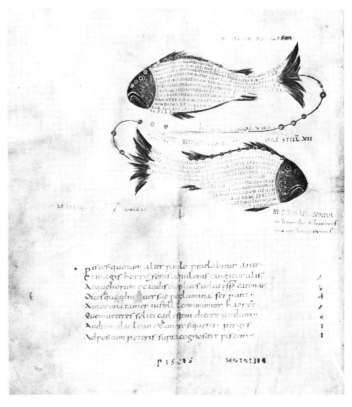

Aratus, a Greek poet (*c*315–*c*245 BC), wrote a long astronomical poem which he called *Phainomena* (it is usually translated as *Things Appearing*). It continued to be read for several centuries in Greek (ABOVE LEFT) and in Latin (ABOVE RIGHT and RIGHT). St Paul quoted from it in a speech to the Athenians (*Acts xvii. 28*). Much of Aratus' astronomical theory came from the well-known observatory of Eudoxus of Cnidus provoke disaster. Free choice meant the right to chose the moment at which to start a project, conceive a child, be born.

There was, by now, a very strong association between certain planets and certain terrestrial events and characteristics. The strongest, of course, was between the Sun and life itself. As one astrologer put it:

The Sun, which nourishes the seeds of all plants, is the first also to gather from them the first fruits as soon as he rises; for this gathering of his uses his rays, if one may employ the term, like immense hands. What indeed are hands for him but those rays that gather in the first place the suavest emanations of plants?

The different quality of sunlight at different times of the day is now a matter of scientific record, here stated with imagery that is specifically Egyptian. Mars is associated by the same ancient astrologer with war, Venus with love, Mercury with speed and messages, and so on. These associations were not only regarded as traditional, but as matters of scientific fact, although the mythical associations between the planets and ancient legend were still preserved, so that Saturn was also Cronos, Jupiter was still Zeus (there is a horoscope dated AD 8, in which Cronos is in the sign of the Bull, Zeus in that of the Crab, Ares (Mars) in that of the Virgin, and so on).

The consensus was that two planets, Jupiter and Venus, were on the whole benevolent, and two were antagonistic, with Mercury neutral. The degree of their influence was geared to their position relative to Earth and the Sun, which was in the middle of the planetary family with Mars, Jupiter and Saturn above, and Venus, Mercury and the Moon below. The lower planets were humid, and colder the further they stood from the Sun. Humidity was thought to be a female element, so the upper planets were believed to be masculine, while Venus and the Moon were feminine, with Mercury a hermaphrodite.

As the astrological theory grew more complex, so it became more difficult to resolve anomalies and confusions; and as astronomy developed it became difficult always to fit the known facts to the mythical characteristics. The zodiac signs, too, caused some confusion; the Greeks saw Aries, for instance, as a character in the legend of the Golden Fleece, while astrologers who had learned from the Chaldeans had to accept it as the Ram of Ammon. Aries naturally tended to preside over the fortunes of wool merchants; but since the Golden Ram lost its fleece, it also tended to provoke sudden disasters in the wool trade!

Despite the fact that there were innumerable difficulties in the way of a practical valuation of the interpretations offered by the astrologers, some people continued to take the subject very seriously indeed – not only the Seleucids, Lagids and Attalids, but smaller states such as Commagene, under King Antiochus I (*c* 80 BC). A former antagonist of Pompey, then his ally in the civil war, who repelled an attack on Samosata by Mark Antony (and Antony, incidentally, is said to have been spied on by an astrologer employed by Cleopatra), Antiochus is interred in a giant tomb on the summit of Nimrud Dagh, 7000 feet above sea level, covered with carvings in relief which provide a fascinating anthology of astrological beliefs of the time. Here Greek and Iranian gods became one: Mithra is Apollo, Ares is Hercules, Zeus is Oromazdes. On the western terrace outside the tomb is a great relief of a lion covered with stars, and with the Moon and three planets: Jupiter near the head, Mercury in the middle and Mars at the tail – the planets associated with Zeus, Apollo and Hercules. This is believed to be a visual interpretation of a horoscope for 6 July 62 BC – the day on which Antiochus was crowned after his reinstatement by Pompey.

As we turn from Greece towards Rome, where astrology really took its place at the very centre of political events, it is to the city of Alexandria that we must look for a sight of the man who drew together all the skeins of astrological thought of his day and did his best to rationalize them in one book. After the death of Alexander, who founded the city, King Ptolemy Soter   Ptolemy I (323–285 BC) – had founded a sort of university at Alexandria, at which the scholars of the city could meet to further their studies. Four hundred years later, the most famous astrologer of ancient times, Claudius Ptolemaeus – Ptolemy – arrived to teach there.

Ptolemy is of course known chiefly as a mathematician, astronomer and geographer, who despite his conviction that the Earth was the centre of the universe around which all other heavenly bodies revolved, devised an astronomical system that was to be adopted by the whole of Europe for centuries. His *Syntaxis* made a great point of insisting on simplicity – no point in inventing complex systems to explain a phenomenon when a simple one would do – and on verification of observation. Astoundingly, without the aid of a telescope, he catalogued 1022 separate stars (compared with the 840 or so catalogued by Hipparchus).

The *Tetrabiblos*, Ptolemy's lengthy astrological textbook, the first really substantial textbook to come down to us complete, is a compilation of the astrological lore of previous centuries, and was written sometime between AD 161 and 139, when he was working in Alexandria. It is in four books, and begins with a rational enough argument: since it is clear that the Sun and Moon have an effect upon terrestrial life (through the seasons, the movements of the tides, and so on), it is surely well to

Ptolemy, or Claudius Ptolemaeus, a native of Egypt who lived at Alexandria, was a great geographer and astronomer. Until recently there was some attempt to argue that his astrological work, the *Tetrabiblos*, was not his own (astrology being considered a study too disreputable for a great man). Present scholarship has however restored it to him

consider the effects the other heavenly bodies may have. Then, in what is admittedly a giant leap, he proposes that

since it is clearly practicable, by an accurate knowledge of the points above enumerated, to make predictions concerning the proper quality of the seasons, there also seems no impediment to the formation of similar prognostications concerning the destiny and disposition of every human being, for ... even at the time of any individual's primary conformation, the general quality of that individual's temperament may be perceived; and the corporeal shape and mental capacity with which the person will be endowed at birth may be pronounced; as well as the favourable and unfavourable events indicated ...

Ptolemy takes what is an extremely realistic view of the subject, despite his obvious partisanship; he admits, for instance, that the science is imperfect, not only because some astrologers are simply bad astrologers, but because there are other influences than astrological ones to be considered. However,

since no weakness is imputed to a physician because he enquires into the individual habit of his patient, as well as into the nature of the disease, no imputation can justly attach to the professor of prognostication because he combines the consideration of species, nurture, education and country with that of the motion of the heavens; for as the physician acts but reasonably in thus considering the proper constitution of the sick person as well as his disease, so, in forming predictions, it must surely be justifiably allowable to comprehend in that consideration every other thing connected with the subject, in addition to the motion of the heavens, and to collect and compare with that motion all other co-operating circumstances arising elsewhere.

Completing Book One of the *Tetrabiblos*, Ptolemy then begins to summarize the workings not only of the Sun, Moon and planets, but of certain fixed stars, going into technical detail. In Book Two, he sets out to 'confine the whole doctrine within the limits of natural reason', delineating two chief areas in which astrology can be of use to man – the general (concerned with entire nations, countries or cities) and the particular (concerning individuals). He relates the dispositions of nations to astrology by pointing out that their people seem to have different temperaments, which can be related to the climate of their countries; such climates being, of course, a matter of the heat of the Sun. The people of the extreme north, for instance, who live 'under the Bears', or close to the arctic circle,

have their zenith far distant from the Zodiac and the Sun's heat. Their constitutions, therefore, abound in cold, and are also highly imbued with moisture, which is in itself a most nutritive quality, and in these latitudes is not exhausted

by heat; hence, they are fair in complexion, with straight hair, of large bodies and full stature. They are cold in disposition, and wild in manners, owing to the constant cold ...

Book Two concludes with a passage on how to interpret eclipses, and on the significance of meteors (which is wholly meteorological). In Book Three, Ptolemy turns to personal astrology. He is clear about the difficulty of obtaining an accurate birth time – let alone the possibility of noting down the correct time of conception. Both depended on astronomical observation, using an astrolabe, or on having a water clock (and even these, he says, have been known to be leaky and therefore inaccurate!). He is not manic about the choice to be made between working from the time of conception or of birth; ideally, both should be noted. But after all,

the conception may in fact be said to be the generation of mere human seed, but the birth that of man himself, since the infant at its birth acquires numerous qualities which it could not possess while in the womb, which are proper to human nature alone.

There are detailed instructions about the interpretation of a birth chart or horoscope, and accounts of just what the good astrologer can expect to be able to discover. The physical appearance is certainly one ingredient. The baby born when Saturn is 'oriental' (or in the eastern half of the birth chart) would be of

a yellowish complexion and a good constitution, with black and curled hair, a broad and stout chest, eyes of ordinary quality, and a proportionate size of body, the temperament of which is compounded principally of moisture and cold. Should he [Saturn] be occidental [in the west of the chart], he makes the personal figure black or dark, thin and small, with scanty hair on the head, the body without hair but well-shaped, the eyes black or dark, and the bodily temperament consisting chiefly of dryness and cold.

Illnesses could be foreseen, and therefore guarded against, by studying the birth chart; so could the qualities of mind of the growing individual. A heavy emphasis on the 'tropical' or 'cardinal' signs (Aries, Cancer, Libra or Capricorn) would

generally dispose the mind to enter much into political matters, rendering it eager to engage in public and turbulent affairs, fond of distinction, and busy in theology; at the same time ingenious, acute, inquisitive, inventive, speculative and studious of astrology and divination.

The 'fixed' signs (Taurus, Leo, Scorpio and Aquarius), if stressed,

make the mind just, uncompromising, constant, firm of purpose, prudent, patient, industrious, strict, chaste, mindful of injuries, steady in pursuing its object, contentious, desirous of honour, seditious, avaricious and pertinacious.

Those born with an emphasis on the 'bicorporeal' or 'mutable' signs, (Gemini, Virgo, Sagittarius or Pisces) would have minds that were

variable, versatile, not easy to be understood, volatile and unsteady, inclined to duplicity, amorous, wily, fond of music, careless, full of expedients, and regretful.

But the planets also play their part in shaping the character. Saturn, for instance, in a certain relationship with Venus in the birth chart, and if 'exalted' (well-placed within a sympathetic sign), made men

averse to women, and renders them fond of governing, prone to solitude, highly reserved, regardless of rank, indifferent to beauty, envious, austere, unsociable, singular in opinion, addicted to divination and to religious services and mysteries, solicitous of the priesthood, fanatical and subservient to religion, solemn, reverential, sedate, studious of wisdom, faithful in friendship, continent, reflective, circumspect, and scrupulous in regard to female friendship.

On the other hand if not in association with Venus, and ill-placed, Saturn could make men licentious and libidinous, practisers of lewdness, careless, and impure in sexual intercourse; obscene, treacherous to women, especially to those of their own families; wanton, quarrelsome, sordid, hating elegance, slanderous, drunken, superstitious, adulterous and impious; blasphemers of the gods and scoffers at holy rites.

Book Four continues the interpretation of various aspects of the birth chart – how to discern a baby's future wealth, rank and employment; the probable nature of his or her marriage, and attitude to sex. For instance Mars placed distantly from Venus and Saturn but in proximity to Jupiter would make men 'pure and decorous in sexual intercourse, and incline them to natural usages only', while if Mars was supported by Venus, they 'will become highly licentious and attempt to gratify their desires in every mode'.

The *Tetrabiblos* was enormously influential in its time, and for centuries after. Other astrologers, such as Hephaestion of Thebes, Paul of Alexandria and Julius Firmicus, used it, and saw it as a seminal work. Even today it is read by astrologers, not merely because some of its precepts are part of astrological heritage, but because it offers cogent arguments to support its theory. For instance, Ptolemy grasped the nettle of the Precession of the Equinoxes, pointing out that 'the beginnings of the signs are to be taken from the equinoctial and tropical points. This rule is not only stated very clearly by writers on the subject, but it is also evident by the demonstrations constantly afforded, that their natures, influences and familiarities have no other origin than from the tropics and equinoxes ... ' In other words, it is the 30 degree section of the ecliptic within which planets may be placed that matters, and not the fact that certain constellations may or may not be behind them. Yet that hoary old argument is still raked up, despite the fact that Ptolemy settled it firmly two thousand years ago.

Some astrologers, who like to view the subject mystically rather than practically, have found Ptolemy somewhat dry and uninspiring. Yet he could be intoxicated, like so many of the astronomers of his time, by the sheer romance of the universe: 'Mortal as I am, I know that I am born for a day; but when I follow the serried multitude of the stars in their circular course, my feet no longer touch the earth; I ascend to Zeus himself to feast me on ambrosia, the food of the gods.'

Ptolemy's sheer enthusiasm no less than his certainty has always been infectious to generations that followed him; but it is also true that many passages of the *Tetrabiblos* read today with a peculiarly modern air, in view of the most recent discoveries of previously unsuspected cosmic rays and gravitational effects between the planets. Its errors of fact are no more (indeed, no less) than those of any scientific treaties of its time; and it is a model of the best of its kind. We have only to compare it with other astrological books of roughly the same period to see its superiority. Take, for instance, the existing fragment of the *Salmeschnaiko*, another influential textbook, full of generalizations:

... This period makes many find their livelihood as advocates, others as wizards, many as singers of gods and kings, and many as translators of languages ... Many, however, also consume the substance of others. [The Lord of Flame] makes many passive homosexuals, and many cohabiting with their aunts and stepmothers so as to debauch them.

It is not easy to discover just how far astrology was used by the Greeks at a personal level. Eudoxos, in the 4th century BC, condemned horoscopes used for personal predictions, and Theophrastus, a little later, was surprised to hear from the Chaldeans that they claimed to be able to predict events in the lives of individuals as well as making weather forecasts. Ennius (239-169 BC) is the first Latin writer to mention the people who

> write down the signs of heaven
> Noting the Goats or Scorpions of great Jove
> And other monstrous names of horrid shapes
> Climbing the Zodiac ...

and Cato, who died in 149 BC, warned the manager of his farm not to consult travelling Chaldeans. Stoicism, when it became the fashion in Rome, must have been responsible for an early interest in astrology, too. It is perhaps fair to guess that the forecasts made for Romans during the early centuries after Christ were of much the same sort as those devised for the Greeks in the centuries before: it is simply that more of the former have survived.

These Roman examples are extremely various, as Jack Lindsay points out in his exhaustive *Origins of Astrology* (1971). Few of them, however, attempt to predict the future. Presumably this was done, if at all, in conversation with clients, and on the basis of lengthy files of notes kept by astrologers, showing the positions of the planets at birth and the subsequent career of the subject, as well as of physical characteristics. A man born on 14 December became a deputy-governor but annoyed his superior and ended up working in a quarry with prisoners. Another, born on 23 April 104, had short arms. Yet another was ill and had a close escape at sea, but was saved thanks to the benevolent position of Saturn.

Most astrologers have kept notes of that sort, building up dossiers relating the positions of the planets at the birth of an individual to subsequent events or to physical characteristics. Someone born on 10 November 114 had in his forty-second year 'quarrels and confusion and notoriety through a woman', and two years later 'the violent death of a slave and crisis of his father, and accusation of ignoble descent and rape. But he received help and gifts from friends ... ' Someone else, born on 21 January 116, was effeminate and 'had unmentionable vices, for Capricorn is lascivious and its ruler [Saturn] was in the Bull, the sign [which would indicate the kind of] weakness, and the Scorpion indicates the kind of lewdery.' Not unsurprisingly, he seems to have been drummed out of his high position in the army after some undefined incident.

By AD 188 Vettius Valens of Antioch, the well-known astrologer, had amassed a fine library of horoscopes, and sets out over a hundred of them in his *Anthologiae*, illustrating the interpretation of birth charts, and stressing that it is as a result of the detailed examination of how the planets have worked in the life of his clients that he has become so practised and accurate an astrologer. His life is the first we have that can be compared to the lives of other professional astrologers throughout the following ages: he continually recorded his findings, occasionally wrote textbooks (his *Teacher's Manual* is, alas, lost), and had continually to defend himself against attacks both from other astrologers and from lay antagonists.

But if many astrologers, through the latter centuries BC in Greece and in the early years of the Roman empire, practised relatively quietly with lay men and women who had only the lowest rank in society, we find for the first time in Rome detailed accounts of the part they played in influencing the politics of a country through high-placed clients. For the next eighteen hundred years astrology was to be part of the personal and political lives of most rulers and of their people.

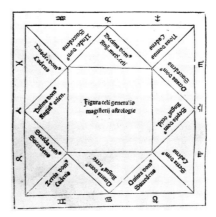

A horoscope from the
Tetrabiblos

IV

THE IMPERIAL PLANETS

TOWARDS the end of the 3rd century BC Greek drama and literature began seriously to interest the Romans. At first, astrology crept in at the lower end of the social scale: while the intelligentsia were enjoying Greek plays and poems, *hoi polloi* was fascinated by the crowds of fortune-tellers making their way – as quacks always will – towards a new source of easy money.

But it was not long before, at first out of an interest in astronomy, intelligent Romans learned about the Greek preoccupation with the influence of the planets on humanity. By the 1st century BC, Cicero, always sceptical about astrology, took it seriously enough to summarize it without irony in his *De divinatione*:

In the starry belt which the Greek calls the Zodiac there is a certain force of such a nature that every part of that belt affects and changes the heavens in a different way, according to the stars that are in this or in an adjoining locality at a given time ... They believe that it is not merely probable, but certain, that just as the temperature of the air is regulated by this celestial force, so also children at their birth are influenced in soul and body, and by this force their minds, manners, disposition, physical condition, career in life and destinies are determined.

Cicero's summary of how astrology worked shows how the intelligent Roman understood the subject: he emphasized that normally only the twelve signs and planets were considered; that it was the ascendant, the rising sign appearing over the eastern horizon at the moment of birth,

OPPOSITE **Ennia Thrasylla**, granddaughter of the astrologer Thrasyllus, was herself an astrologer, and the Emperor Caligula (here the centre of a decorative ceiling by Mantegna) was her influential lover

OPPOSITE The astrologer Balbillus became a close friend of the Emperor Claudius, whose mother described him as 'a man whom Mother Nature began work on, then cast aside', and so probably less prepossessing than this magnificent statue in Rome

that was the 'natal sign' (not the 'Sun sign', which was not to become strongly associated with simplistic astrology until the 20th century); that the astrologer drew his conclusions from the angles between the planets as they were placed in the twelve constellations, and in the 'houses', each of which showed an influence in one area of the life of the subject – house four was that of the parents, house five that of children, house ten of honours and house eleven of friends.

We are not concerned here with the growth of the star cults among the Romans between 300 and 150 BC; but during those years various new divinities took up residence, among them Asclepius, Cybele, Bacchus, Isis and Mithras (to say nothing of Jehovah); they all, however, had to some extent astrological associations (even Jehovah), and contributed to a growth of serious interest in the subject. Mithras, especially, took that interest out into the Empire, making converts abroad: 'modern' astrology undoubtedly first reached Britain in the form of Zodiacal carvings at Mithraic shrines, while Asclepius became the patron saint of astrological medicine.

As is usually the case when a country is invaded by a new culture, some reactionaries took great exception to the changing times. But the tide was

RIGHT The Roman Army spread the cult of Mithras, a Sun god, throughout the lands it conquered. A carving from the Mithraeum discovered in London shows Mithras, typically, as a beautiful youth driving a sword into the neck of a bull, which at the same time is being attacked by a scorpion and a dog. And surrounding the tableau is a zodiac against them. Scipio Africanus, for instance, the conqueror of Hannibal, whose scandalous interest in things Greek was said to have persuaded him to go about in public in Greek dress, was a great upholder of phil-hellenism; and even the sceptical and strong-minded Cato, towards the end of his life, was infected with the new spirit, and started to learn Greek.

It was Cato who quite properly issued warnings about the innumerable quack astrologers and magicians coming to Rome in and around 200-150 BC. The poet Ennius, a southern Italian brought to Rome by Cato, attacked them too:

> Of little use are these Marsian quacks,
> Village-astrologers and fortune-tellers
> In crowded circuses, or priests of Isis,
> Pretend-interpreters of all your dreams.
> These lying conjurers have not the skill
> To read the future; just a pack of hypocrites
> Prompted by hunger, they don't know themselves
> Let alone others; yet they'll promise you
> Enormous fortunes - if you'll share with them!

But the influence of the quack astrologers was far outweighed by the influence of the knowledge accumulated by Greek astronomers, and the Romans were enormously impressed by scientific achievements. When Marcellus conquered Syracuse in 212 BC, and returned to Rome with a magnificent model of the celestial spheres which he had found in the house of Archimedes (killed when the city fell), it was greatly admired – and used. And since the two terms were still synonymous (*astronomia* is sometimes used where we, today, would expect to find *astrologia*, and vice versa – Plato uses only *astronomia*, Aristotle only *astrologia*) this meant there was at the least increased pressure on intelligent Romans to look at the theory that the planets affected human behaviour.

A minority declined to be persuaded: Cicero, as we have seen, but also, a century earlier, the Greek sceptic philosopher Carneades. He was one of the heads of the Platonic Academy, and ambassador from Athens to Rome in 156 BC. He maintained that not only was it virtually impossible to make an accurate observation of the sky at the moment of birth (let alone conception), but that it was clear that astrology did not and could not work because people born at the same moment could have very different destinies, while others born at very different times and places died at precisely the same time; moreover, animals would have the same fate as human beings whose birth moment they shared, and people of different races, customs and creeds born at the same moment would obviously have different fates. He failed to see that his second and last

The Romans enthusiastically adapted astrology to enrich the pantheon of their gods: here, some of those gods are shown, with the zodiacal correspondences – Jupiter and Taurus, Venus and Gemini, Ceres and Virgo

objections cancelled each other out: most astrologers then as now made it quite clear that astrology was only one ingredient of a life, and environment and custom would certainly mitigate its effect.

Carneades' objections have been rehearsed many times since his first statement of them (among others, by St Augustine, who took them wholesale and used them as his own). They are on the whole not very convincing, although they had more significance at the time they were made, when some astrologers at least were highly fatalistic. And certainly they must have had an effect in Rome, where Carneades was sensationally successful as a lecturer – fashionable young Romans eager to keep up with Greek culture and fashion crowded the halls in which he spoke.

It would be a mistake to assume, then, that astrology had a walk-over. In 139 BC, an edict was actually passed enabling Rome to expel any foreigner who gave trouble; the arguments of Carneades were used to support the claim that astrologers were simply exploiting the credulous poor, and many of them were thrown out. The attitude of authority – that astrology seemed likely to cause trouble – was borne out in 134-2 BC, when there was a sizeable slave revolt in Sicily, led by one Eunus, who either was or gave an inspired imitation of being an astrologer. He was obviously a very accomplished charlatan (if we are to believe the historian Florus, who says that among his tricks was the concealment of a nut full of sulphur in his mouth, which flamed with fire and smoke as he spoke), and with the aid of tricks and oratory commanded the force of over 60,000 slaves. Even when the rebellion was crushed, the Romans were sufficiently impressed with Eunus as a seer to capture him alive.

Less than thirty years later, Athenio, another astrologer (this time a serious one) led another slave revolt in Sicily; insisting that the planets had revealed that he was to be king of Sicily, he and his followers gave trouble until about 100 BC, when he was killed in a hand-to-hand fight with the consul Manius Aquillius.

The first real Roman astrological expert was one Publius Nigidius Figulus – not a mere nobody, but someone who held public office, as an *aedile* and later as *praetor*, or magistrate. His reputation as an astrologer was considerable, and he was at the centre of what was virtually the earliest Roman astrological school, and among other books published several on prediction and meteorology, as well as on pure astronomy. Alas, Julius Caesar, when he came to power, was unsympathetic, and banished him (although probably for political rather than astrological reasons).

The growth of public interest is illustrated in the work of M. Terentius Varro, a colleague of Nigidius Figulus – not himself an astrologer, but keenly interested in the subject as a means of clarifying history. He commissioned a horoscope of Rome itself and its founder, Romulus – the first example we have of astrology being used to reveal the past by examining the history of a person or place, and from this estimating the probable 'birth time'. Cicero reports that Lucius Tarutius of Firmum, a mutual friend, calculated that Rome was 'born' when the Moon was in Libra, and 'from that fact unhesitatingly prophesied our destiny'. Plutarch later reported Tarutius' findings in greater detail, suggesting that 'these and similar speculations will perhaps attract readers by their novelty and extravagance rather than offend them by their fabulous character.'

Varro, although not an astrologer, included a chapter on astrology in his *De disciplinus* which was so good and so economically expressed that it was used and used again by later writers. One of his friends seems to have been that C. Fonteius Capito who went with Antony to the East, and played an important part in reconciling him, briefly, with Octavianus before returning to Egypt to travel with Cleopatra to Syria.

The sceptics were thinning out, and fighting a by no means successful rearguard action. Cicero remained unconvinced, even after a stay on Rhodes with the Greek Stoic Posidonius, and a close friendship with Nigidius Figulus. He seems to tolerate the idea of astrology in his *On my consulate*, but later unequivocally states his opinion that 'the condition of the heavenly bodies may, if you will, influence some things, but it certainly will not influence everything.' He was not silly enough to deny that the Sun influenced the growth of plants, or the Moon the tides, but was very doubtful about any effect the planets might have on human life. And still later, in his essay *On divination*, he pressed the attack, giving eight specific criticisms, including the old question of the birth of twins, the possibility of astrologers not being able properly to see the sky, and the effect of environment – also bringing in the fact that 'the parental seed' contributed to a person's appearance, habits and outlook, and that the new advances in medicine meant that 'natural defects' with which a child might be born could be cured. *On divination* is perhaps the coolest example of early Roman scepticism; another occurs in Lucretius' poem *De rerum natura*, in which he argues in favour of free will, and that the soul is as mortal as the body, and thus no celestial panacea is acceptable.

Among the myths perpetuated by some astrological historians is that representing Julius Caesar as a proponent of astrology, or even himself an astrologer. On the contrary, he seems to have been almost entirely sceptical, although he accepted the obvious planetary effect on weather and plant growth. Otherwise, he not only rejected old-fashioned omens, but at least two horoscopes presented to him by celebrated astrologers promising him a happy and peaceful death at the height of years of success. Perhaps the legends of his interest in the subject arose because of his choice of the symbol of the Bull as his legionary standard (Taurus is 'ruled' by Venus, and Venus herself was said to be Caesar's ancestress). Most likely, he chose this deliberately, pandering to the superstition of the ordinary soldiers. There seems to be no reason to reject the story that tells of his refusing to accept his wife Calpurnia's warning dream of the night before his death; and it seems, too, to be a fact that an astrologer called Spurinna warned him to 'beware the Ides of March'.

He seems to have known Spurinna quite well; he mentions him in his letters. It seems likely that it was this astrologer who, in 46 BC, had advised Caesar against crossing to Africa until after the winter solstice – advice Caesar rejected, and without catastrophe. Cicero knew him well, too, and scorned his abilities. Well, he was accurate enough when he

Augustus the Venerable, the Magnificent, Emperor of Rome, as a youth visited anonymously an astrologer called Theogenes – who, on hearing his birth data, rose and threw himself at his visitor's feet. This gave Augustus such confidence in his destiny that he published his own horoscope. However, he took the precaution of pretending to be a Capricornian (and thus disciplined, ambitious, prudent) rather than the Libran he really was (and therefore indecisive, changeable and gullible!)

warned Caesar that he 'should beware a danger which would not threaten him beyond the Ides of March', as Plutarch reported it; and Cassius Dio, the Roman historian of AD *c* 150-235, pointed out that here was a good example of the fateful nature of a firm astrological prediction.

At Caesar's death, a splendidly showy comet appeared, to blaze through the night sky for seven consecutive evenings; clearly he had become immortal, and was on his way to shine among the stars.

During his student days at Apollonia, when he was regarded as certain to be the next monarch, Octavianus Augustus had visited a well-known local astrologer, Theogenes, who, the moment he set eyes on Octavianus' birth chart, threw himself at the young man's feet. Unsurprisingly, Octavianus was extremely impressed, and (so Suetonius says) 'from that time on had such faith in his destiny that he made his horoscope public and issued a silver coin stamped with the sign of the constellation Capricorn under which he was born.'

At all events, Octavianus saw in the public reaction to the appearance of Caesar's comet in 44 BC the fact that astrology could be a fine implement of public relations. But only if it was on his side – and most of the astrologers in Rome at the time of Caesar's death tended to favour the fortunes of Antony, whose identification with the East (and indeed with Cleopatra) appealed to them. Octavianus made Agrippa (a lifelong friend who had been with him on that visit to Theogenes) *aedile*, and instructed him to expel from the city all astrologers and sorcerers.

He was no doubt right. By now, very few men at any level of intelligence or society contested the skills of the astrologers. Vitruvius, the great architect, reflected in his book the attitude of most people: everyone must, he said, accept the calculations of 'the Chaldeans', who could explain the past and future from astronomical calculations. He was completely assured that astrology worked, and as a science. Other authors of the time support this view: Horace, Virgil, Propertius, Ovid. And by now it appears that the Emperor Augustus (as Octavianus was proclaimed) shared it.

In the first place, he sought the advice of astrologers about a possible marriage for his only child, Julia. His stepsons Tiberius and Drusus were in their teens, and Julia herself only 16; obviously the sooner she was safely married, the better. The astrologers recommended Marcellus, Julia's first cousin. Consumptive and weakly, the boy died within two years of the wedding. The astrological advisers had better luck, of a sort, the second time. Advised by them, Augustus persuaded his friend Agrippa to divorce his wife and marry Julia. The marriage lasted eleven years and produced a clutch of possible heirs, although none of them in fact succeeded.

In 12 BC, Augustus once more ordered measures against the astrologers who had crept back into Rome during the past twenty-five years or so. Many of them were publishing predictions about the succession, some worryingly hare-brained. The Emperor passed a law submitting all prophesies to censorship; most of them perished in the flames before they reached the public.

Much of the astrological speculation hinged on a possible third marriage for the notoriously immoral Julia. Now, Augustus ordered his elder stepson Tiberius to divorce a much-loved wife and marry Julia. There was nothing Tiberius could do but comply – unless, of course, he chose suicide. A successful soldier, Tiberius managed to get away from Julia to go campaigning – gaining great honour. But when opportunities for this failed, and he could stand his new wife no longer, he asked Augustus' permission to retire to Rhodes 'to study'. The Emperor, who on principle disbelieved anything horrid he heard about his daughter, coldly agreed; so, in 6 BC, Tiberius went to Rhodes, and the general opinion was that, as a possible successor to the Emperor, he was finished.

Rhodes was a lonely place for a man straight from the centre of the Empire. Tiberius occupied his time gloomily attending classes given by local scholars, and at one of them met the man who was to become, with him, one of the two most important men in Rome: Thrasyllus, an Alexandrian grammarian, editor of Plato and Democritus, and an astrologer. There are various legends about the manner of that first meeting: that, for instance, Tiberius sought out many astrologers for their opinion about his future, killing them immediately they had interpreted his horoscope. Thrasyllus was the only one to comment on his own danger, which impressed Tiberius so much that he spared him. This is probably nonsense. But that is not to say that Tiberius was not impressed by Thrasyllus' first-rate mind, and it certainly seems true that he taught Tiberius how to set up and interpret a horoscope, and successfully predicted that he would soon be recalled to Rome and a bright future. When this happened – when Augustus sent for Tiberius in AD 4 and officially proclaimed him his heir – Thrasyllus travelled with him, and on reaching Rome received from his patron the valuable gift of Roman citizenship.

Ten years later, after a decade during which Thrasyllus ingratiated himself not only with his Emperor but with Roman society, Augustus died – his death accompanied, if we are to believe Cassius Dio, by a total eclipse of the Sun, a display of fire and glowing embers falling from the sky, and a number of melancholy comets. Tiberius was now Emperor, and Thrasyllus the power behind the throne.

Tiberius' reign lasted for nine years, and during it Thrasyllus was never far from his side. It is clear that he not only advised him on day-to-day matters, but about his close friends and the members of his family. By now, the astrologer had consolidated his status in Rome. His wife, who seems to have been called Aka, and to have been a minor princess of Commagene, had also been awarded Roman citizenship, and he had managed to arrange a Roman marriage for his daughter Claudia. Her husband was a Roman knight, L. Ennius, and they eventually had a daughter, Ennia Thrasylla, who was herself to become famous if not notorious.

Very few citizens of Rome during the reigns of the majority of Emperors were entirely free of fear, and Tiberius was by no means the least cruel or capricious. Thrasyllus was as safe as anyone; some other astrologers must have slept less comfortably. When in AD 16, Scribonius

The Emperor Tiberius forbade astrologers to predict death, but relied implicitly on the advice of Thrasyllus, perhaps the most powerful astrologer ever to have been attached to a ruler. The historian Suetonius says that Tiberius 'lacked any deep regard for the gods or other religious feelings, his belief in astrology having persuaded him that the world was wholly ruled by fate'. During storms, he commonly wore a laurel wreath, which he believed would protect him from lightning

Libo, a slightly dense *praetor*, attempted to organize a coup against the Emperor, and took the advice of two astrologers – L. Pituanius and P. Marcius – they were arrested with him; the first was thrown from the Tarpeian rock, and the second stripped naked outside the Esquiline Gate, his head fixed in a forked stake, and beaten to death.

Some other people suffered because of a mere interest in astrology. In AD 20, Aemilia Lepida, a woman of good family, once the fiancée of Augustus' grandson, was exiled for consulting an astrologer (although also on suspicion of trying to poison a former husband).

During the early years of Tiberius' reign a complex situation arose which Thrasyllus succeeded in riding like a wave. This concerned the Emperor's son Drusus, who seems (with reason) to have been jealous of Thrasyllus' influence with his father. When in the early 20s the Emperor's favourite, the *praetor* Sejanus, started a tempestuous affair with Drusus' wife Livilla, the lovers seem to have consulted Thrasyllus about their actions. Whether or not he played any part in the subsequent poisoning of Drusus, we cannot know. But Thrasyllus was left with the problem whether to support Sejanus or betray him and Livilla to the Emperor. There seems no question that the astrologer played a vital part in Tiberius' decision to leave Rome in 26, never to live there again; and this meant that Thrasyllus could maintain his influence with both Tiberius and Sejanus, supporting the latter in the battle for the succession which had arisen between him and Agrippina, Augustus' granddaughter, who wanted the throne for her children.

Sejanus, although rising higher and higher in Tiberius' estimation, continually sought to destroy opposition that might stand between him and the succession. He organized the trial of Agrippina and her son Nero for high treason, banishing one to Pandataria and the other to Pontia. And Thrasyllus further consolidated *his* position by marrying his granddaughter Ennia to Naevius Sertorius Macro, gaining another Roman knight as a close relative by marriage.

Whether Thrasyllus consulted the planets and was prompted by them to engineer a plot against Sejanus, or was simply consulting his own interests without astrological persuasion, he was certainly at the centre of such a plot; his son-in-law Macro not only carried the orders that destroyed Sejanus, but immediately took his place at the centre of Roman life, while Tiberius remained in self-imposed exile on Capri.

There, with him, lived Agrippina's younger son Caius; and it was this youth who now received Thrasyllus' support as successor to the throne. We know that Tiberius time and time again talked with his astrologer about the succession, and the evidence is that time and time again

Thrasyllus persuaded him that the planets revealed that Caius could never succeed – that 'he had as much chance of becoming Emperor as he had of driving his racing chariot across the Bay of Baiae'. By this means he prevented the perverse Emperor from legally disqualifying Caius from the succession. What Caius felt about this is uncertain, except that we hear that he vowed that one of the first things he would do when he gained the throne would be to drive his chariot across the waters of Baiae.

Thrasyllus' relationship with the old, irritable and nervous Emperor was now extremely tricky. It is not easy to conjecture to what extent he honestly relied on his astrological knowledge, and to what extent concern for his own safety and that of his friends led him to equivocate. He did not hesitate to advise the Emperor to continue to trust the consul Servius Galba, for instance, although at his birth Thrasyllus had told Tiberius that Galba's horoscope showed signs that he would reach the heights of commanding power. Now, he reassured the Emperor that Galba's horoscope showed he would only become Emperor in old age – which meant Tiberius was probably safe from him. It is also clear that Thrasyllus could only advise the Emperor on the basis of genuine astrological calculations, for Tiberius himself was quite capable of these, and would have seen through any pretence.

This presents the problem of Thrasyllus' advice to Tiberius, given it seems in about AD 34, that he still had ten years of healthy life ahead of him. It has been taken for granted that Thrasyllus falsified the horoscope in some way, in order to prevent the ever-increasing number of judicial and non-judicial murders the Emperor was undertaking to protect himself against the ambitious. But Tiberius knew his own horoscope backwards; if Thrasyllus foresaw that he would in fact die within three years, he must have found some way of persuading his client otherwise.

In fact, Thrasyllus was to predecease Tiberius – although not before one final concern, when he learned that his daughter Ennia, on a visit to Capri, had started an adulterous affair with Caius, now fairly clearly the main contender for the throne after Tiberius' death. Macro, Ennia's husband, may or may not have known about the affair; he was by this time almost as unpopular as Sejanus had been at the height of his power, and neither his position nor Ennia's could have given Thrasyllus much comfort in the few months before his death – which he is said to have foretold to the hour.

Ironically, even after his death, Thrasyllus preserved the life of one of the earth's monsters, the Emperor Nero. Tiberius, continuing to ensure his own safety and juggle with the succession, had arranged several trials of alleged conspirators against the throne; and at the time of his death

The Emperor Nero was born, according to Suetonius, just as the Sun was rising, so that 'his earliest rays touched the newly-born boy almost before he could be laid on the ground, as the custom was ...' When his birth chart was drawn up, his horoscope was revealed as forbidding and ominous. During his reign he was said to have slaughtered the chief nobility of Rome to propitiate a comet which an astrologer warned him was an evil omen

those awaiting trial included Domitius Ahenobarbus, the husband of Agrippina the Younger. When the Emperor died, Domitius was released from prison, and went home to his wife – who nine months later gave birth to the baby Nero. Had Thrasyllus not assured Tiberius that his life was safe for at least another decade, the trials would swiftly have been concluded, Domitius executed, and Nero would never have been born. (As it was, Suetonius says that the astrologer who calculated the baby's horoscope almost fainted away on contemplating its horrendous nature!)

Rome now had a new Emperor, Caius, who called himself Caligula. A considerable amount of carnage followed his accession, and among those who fled from Rome to avoid this was Thrasyllus' alleged son, Tiberius Claudius Balbillus. (Jack Lindsay, in *Origins of astrology*, 1971, argues that Balbillus was no relation of Thrasyllus; but we know that the latter's son was called 'Tiberius Claudius', and the relationship seems a likely one.) He settled in Alexandria, while his niece Ennia, whose lover was now on the throne, stayed to enjoy what seemed likely to be a position of considerable influence. Caligula is said to have given Ennia a written contract promising to marry her after becoming Emperor. If she relied on this, she was a less keen judge of human nature than her grandfather. Her husband Macro, who had done much to help Caligula to the throne, was killed on the Emperor's orders, and she apparently committed suicide. Not long after hearing of her death, Caligula married Lollia Paulina, who eleven years later was herself executed for consulting astrologers, allegedly to organize a coup against the Emperor Claudius.

Although Caligula continued to uphold the edict Augustus had laid down in AD 11, forbidding any astrologer to consult an Emperor's horoscope, his death was foretold by an Egyptian called Apollonius, who was hauled off to Rome and (according to Cassius Dio) sentenced to die on the very day he had said would be the Emperor's last. Foolishly, Caligula postponed the execution, the better to say 'I told you so'; but the Emperor died at the foretold time, assassinated on 24 January in AD 41.

Now Claudius became Emperor, and it was safe for Balbillus to return to Rome, for Claudius when a boy had been a constant visitor to Thrasyllus' house, and with an interest in intellectual matters uncommon in his family, had enjoyed hearing about literature and astrology, and enjoyed too the company of Balbillus, who he now received with enthusiasm. When in 43 he went to help conquer Britain, Balbillus went too, as an officer in the 20th legion – not only to give astrological advice, but to help run the engineers' corps. Claudius on his return to Rome was honoured with the title Britannicus; Balbillus received a crown of honour. He seems then to have split his time between Rome and Alexandria, for he was appointed high priest of the Temple of Hermes there, and also became head of the state university with its superb library (where he instituted an annual series of lectures in honour of Claudius, at which the Emperor's own works were recited).

Balbillus became, indeed, as respected a figure as his father – although he tried to keep clear of politics. The part he played in advising Claudius is obscure, but it is likely that he was behind at least one edict – that which announced, before the event, that there would be an eclipse of the Moon on one of the Emperor's birthdays. Much superstition still attached to eclipses, and it was wise to allay in advance any public fears that this one might be a malevolent omen.

Claudius was (no doubt encouraged by Balbillus) quite aware of the harm that could be done by intriguers who cared to use astrology to suggest good times at which to organize insurrection or even assassination. In 52, Furius Camillus Scribonianus was executed for alleged plotting against the Emperor; the evidence included a horoscope of Claudius found in his possession. Soon afterwards Claudius passed an edict, which, like the one in 16, banished all astrologers from the country. The very next year, one T. Statilius Taurus committed suicide after being accused of 'divination'. Two years later Domitia Lepida was accused of using black magic against Agrippina; astrology was mentioned at her trial, too (as at most similar trials).

Balbillus, like his father, found it impossible to avoid politics altogether, particularly the intrigues that now began to centre around the ambitions of two mothers – Agrippina the Younger, who wanted the throne for Nero, and Domitia, her sister-in-law, who wanted it for Claudius' son Britannicus. Agrippina had been told by Balbillus in 41 that Nero would be Emperor, but would murder his mother. This did not dissuade her, and pursuing her ambition she managed to marry Claudius, becoming his fourth wife (his third, Messalina, having met an unpleasant end).

Another astrologer now joined the court: Chaeremon, from Alexandria, known for his assertion that comets could presage joy as well as disaster. He was joined by the Stoic philosopher Lucius Annaeus Seneca, himself an adherent of astrology. The three were mainly responsible for the education of Nero. There seems little doubt that Balbillus took part in the extraordinary events after Claudius' death when Agrippina personally prevented Britannicus from leaving his room until, at an auspicious moment proposed by astrologers, Nero could be, and was, proclaimed Emperor. Balbillus was rewarded by being appointed Prefect of Egypt, where he stayed until 59.

Not long after his return, in 64, the fire that destroyed Rome while Nero allegedly played his fiddle spawned sufficient discontent to result in a plot to destroy the Emperor. When a spectacular comet appeared, Balbillus told Nero that it presaged disaster for him – unless he deflected its effects by executing some of the noblest men of Rome by way of sacrifice. In the following carnage Petronius, who had directed the entertainments at Nero's court, Seneca and his brother, his nephew the poet Lucanus, and many others perished. Balbillus did not. His success, if that is what it was, also made him secure against that dangerous rival astrologer, Ptolemy, the favourite of the new Empress Poppaea. Nero disposed of the rival by killing his wife in a fit of drunken pique. Balbillus retired quietly from the scene, vanishing from sight during the years when Nero died and Galba, Otho and Vitellius acceded and fell in their turn.

It was probably as well; it has always been said that among Nero's many victims towards the end of his reign were a number of astrologers – and certainly several Romans who had somehow got hold of the Imperial horoscope, for Nero supposed that the only reason for its possession was an assassination plot.

Galba, who succeeded Nero, had been told by Tiberius on the evidence of his horoscope that he would one day be Emperor, but he does not seem to have been uncommonly impressed by astrology. Otho is said by Tacitus to have plotted against Galba with the support of astrologers who 'urged him to action, predicting from their observation of the heavens, revolutions and a year of glory'. Ptolemy Seleucus positively ordered Otho to seize the propitious moment, and was proved right: Galba was successfully killed, and Otho ascended the throne. However, the Roman legions in Germany had proclaimed Vitellius Emperor, in the face of whose determined assault Otho crumpled, and killed himself.

Vitellius was not a follower of the planets, perhaps because the horoscope cast for him revealed that although he would become Emperor after a civil war, his reign would be brief. He continually said he did not believe this; and indeed it was a remarkable prediction to make, for there seemed little chance of its coming true. However, he did become Emperor (in 69), and although he expelled all astrologers by an edict passed a few days afterwards, and executed a number of them, he reigned only for three months.

During that short reign, Ptolemy Seleucus, who had got safely out of Rome, threw in his lot with Vespasian, plotting an uprising against Vitellius. Despite the fact that a comet appeared and two eclipses took place (to say nothing of the fact that several people saw two suns in the sky at the same time) Vespasian succeeded in becoming Emperor. This was a good time for Balbillus to return from self-imposed exile, for he and Vespasian had been on good terms since they met at Nero's court (where Vespasian endeared himself to posterity by falling asleep during one of Nero's recitations, a comment that happily escaped the Emperor's notice).

Vespasian was as devoted to astrology as some of his predecessors. On the evidence of Cassius Dio, he 'consulted all the best of them', and not only showed special interest in what Balbillus had to say, but allowed games to be held at Ephesus in the astrologer's honour – the Great Balbillean Games were held until well into the 3rd century. He trusted Balbillus, and indeed Ptolemy Seleucus, so implicitly that when it was discovered that Mettius Pompusianus, an ambitious Roman, had been bruiting it about that he was destined to be Emperor, Vespasian actually had him appointed to the consulate, so sure was he that his own astrologers were right when they said that Mettius had been wrongly advised.

Balbillus may have died at about the same time as Vespasian; had he survived there is no reason why the new Emperor, Vespasian's son Titus, should not have retained him, but his name vanished from record. Titus reigned for only two years, and in 81 was succeeded by his younger brother Domitian, who himself was so convinced by an astrologer's prediction that he would die by iron that he refused the senate's offer of a guard of honour to escort him with spears. For safety's sake, he appears to have believed *all* astrological predictions on principle. He executed Mettius Pompusianus, believing the prophesy that he would one day be Emperor, and Suetonius says that 'he had not failed to take careful note of the days and hours when the foremost men had been born, and as a result was destroying in advance not a few who did not feel the least hope of gaining power.' At least two astrologers seem to have predicted the hour of Domitian's death, and Suetonius says that as the stated hour approached the Emperor became more and more nervous. On 17 September 96, he told his servants to set aside some truffles for him until next day – in case he was around to eat them, for his death had been foretold for the 18th, when 'the Moon in Aquarius will be stained with blood'. He summoned the astrologer Ascletarius-Asclation and asked him if he could foresee his own death. The astrologer replied that he would be torn to pieces by dogs. Domitian had him executed immediately; but as the body was awaiting cremation, a sudden rainstorm put out the fire, the undertaker took shelter, and a pack of dogs destroyed the corpse. Early next morning the second astrologer, Larginus Proculus, was brought before Domitian in chains. Domitian ordered his execution, too, but following Caligula's example postponed this for twenty-four hours, in order that Larginus should see how wrong he had been.

It was at the fifth hour that the two astrologers had said Domitian would die. Nervously, Domitian again and again sent to know the time. Finally his bored servants assured him that the hour had passed, and the Emperor, much relieved, decided to bathe. A conspirator, Stephanus, asked if he could read to him for a while in the bath. Domitian agreed. Whereupon Stephanus produced a dagger and stabbed him, a number of other conspirators rushing in to join the execution.

V

THE PERVASIVE PLANETS

ALTHOUGH astrology failed to play as influential a part in the life of any emperor during the last three centuries of the history of Imperial Rome as it had in the lives of, say, Tiberius or Nero, it did not suffer an eclipse.

On the contrary, it remained an absolutely integral part of Roman life. Sufficient horoscopes have survived to show that anyone with the means to consult an astrologer did so as a matter of course. Some of them tell us in considerable detail about the lives and ambitions, weaknesses and strengths of ordinary citizens. Apart from that, there were public manifestations of a general interest in the constellations and the planets: the huge eagle of Zeus on the ceiling of the sanctuary of Bel at Palmyra, for instance, was surrounded by the zodiac; at the races, chariots were started from stalls, each one of which bore a sign of the zodiac, and then raced around a circuit where each course represented that of one of the seven planets (hot competition, no doubt, for the one representing Mercury!). Even the division of the year into weeks of seven days, each subordinate to one of the planets, indicates how deep-rooted was the idea that the meaning of the universe was somehow geared to the movement of the planets in their courses.

The imagery of astrology was everywhere. One of the most famous examples is the feast described by Petronius in the *Satyricon*, given by the freedman Trimalchio, who sat his guests around a table on which various dishes were set out under the signs of the zodiac - beef under Taurus, sweetbreads and kidneys under Gemini, a balance with a tart on one scale and a cheesecake on the other under Libra, two mullets under Pisces, and so on.

Juvenal mentions several instances of people consulting astrologers, and although he was given to satirical exaggeration, we get a very firm impression of how the upper echelons of Roman society employed them: children would enquire about the time when their parents might be expected to die, women whether their lovers would survive them, and some people positively would not stir abroad without an astrological consultation:

Remember to avoid the tracks of women in whose hands you see (as if they were large gems) much-used ephemerides [tables of planetary movements]. Such a woman does not consult any astrologers; she is herself consulted. Nor will she accompany her husband when he goes to camp, or returns home, if warned against doing so by the numerical manual of Thrasyllus. She will not even go out as far as the first milestone unless a favourable hour has been chosen first from the book. When the rubbed corner of her eye itches, she will ask for a soothing balm only after consulting her horoscope. She may lie in bed sick; then no hour will be considered more apt for taking some food than the one which Petosiris has named . . .

For those who found astrology suspect, and were properly outraged by the superstitious dependence upon it of the unthinking, there came something of a respite for a year or two after AD 96, when Nerva succeeded Domitian as Emperor; although the senators are said to have consulted his horoscope before electing him, his interest in the subject was marginal. Trajan, who succeeded Nerva in 98, was even less interested, although he seems to have been in touch with the grandson of Balbillus, who turned up in Athens. C. Julius Antiochus Epiphanes Philopappus (the ruins of whose monument still stand in Athens) was born during Nero's reign, and grew up safely at the court of his paternal grandfather Antiochus IV, last King of Commagene, at Samosata. Trajan not only made Philopappus a member of the imperial guard, but a consul. The nature of their relationship is unknown, however.

With the accession of Hadrian in 117, astrology once more approached the throne – indeed, mounted it, for the new Emperor was himself an astrologer, whose interest in the subject seemed to stem from his early teens, spent studying Greek and Roman culture in Rome, before being sent into the army by his guardian Trajan. He cordially disliked army life, and consulted at least two astrologers to ask for confirmation of the prediction apparently made at his birth, when his great-uncle Aelius Hadrianus, an astrologer, had promised he would one day be emperor. Confirmation was enthusiastically given.

An amateur astrologer, Aelius Hadrianus, forecast that his grandson would become Emperor of Rome. The grandson, the Emperor Hadrian, perhaps not surprisingly consulted astrologers all his life, and used them in attempting to choose a successor to the throne

Hadrian is the first Roman emperor whose complete horoscope has survived (in several manuscript copies among a selection of horoscopes kept by Antigonus of Nicaea, where they were found by Hephaestion of Thebes in the 4th century). We know that Hadrian was born with the Sun, Moon and Jupiter in Aquarius, Saturn and Mercury in Capricorn, Venus and Mars in Pisces - suggesting, among other things, great ambition and a preoccupation with power, arrogance and obstinacy, a high sense of justice, and a tendency to be ruled entirely by the emotions in personal relationships, which would tend to be unconventional. Interestingly, those with the Moon in Aquarius are traditionally said to have a flair for astrology.

Hadrian drew up his own horoscope and consulted it regularly; he is said to have written down on the first of January each year the major events of his life for the following twelve months, and to have predicted the time of his death to the hour. He was intensely superstitious, and interested in all forms of divination. His empress, Sabina, had rather a chill time of it, childless and rejected by her husband in favour of such beautiful young men as Antinous, who he even took with him on his last great ceremonial tour to Athens, on through Asia Minor to Egypt, and back to Italy through Syria and Athens again. Sabina was comforted on that tour by the presence of her lady-in-waiting and friend Julia Balbilla, a considerable poet, and none other than the great-granddaughter of Thrasyllus, who being the descendant of a king and a Roman knight was on easy terms with her mistress.

We do not know whether Julia had an interest in astrology greater than the normal; nor do we know whether Hadrian or any of his consultant astrologers foretold the central event of the tour – the death of Antinous by drowning in the Nile. There is a dark hint in Cassius Dio that Antinous may have sacrificed himself, or even perhaps have been sacrificed, because an astrologer had foretold the Emperor's own death unless someone of importance elected to die for him (remember, Balbillus had told Nero in 64 that only by killing some of Rome's noblemen could he escape death). Certainly his astrologers tried to console Hadrian by pointing to the convenient 'new' star as the soul of his favourite, now shining in heaven. Astronomers still refer to Antinoos.

When Hadrian fell mortally ill in 136, interest in the succession focused on two men: Lucius Ceionius Commodus who, as Aelius Verus, he proclaimed his official successor, and Pedanius Fuscus, who at his birth had been stamped by astrologers as a coming emperor. At the time when Aelius Verus was proclaimed, he was already too ill to make a speech of thanks to the senate, and it seems that Hadrian was relying on a horoscope (drawn up either by himself or someone else) which had promised him a long life. When an astrologer suggested to the Emperor that there was some mistake – the wrong birth time had been used, perhaps – Hadrian answered: 'It is easier for you to say that when you are looking for an heir to your property, rather than to the empire.' Anyway, Aelius Verus died before Hadrian, who was left with the necessity of making another choice.

This fell upon Antoninus Pius, on condition that he adopted L. Verus (Aelius Verus' son) and an older boy, Marcus Aurelius, as his own heirs. Pedanius Fuscus was outraged, foolishly became involved in a plot to seize the throne, and was arrested and executed. A surviving horoscope by Antigonus of Nicaea says that he 'was born to become, at the age of 25, the cause of his own destruction and that of his parents', and gives the reasons for his fall – which include his being ill-advised because Mercury

Under the Emperor Antonius Pius the mint at Alexandria issued many coins with astrological symbols (this one bears Leo, the lion)

and Saturn were in a male sign, being discovered in a plot because the Moon was in Scorpio, and dying because Mars and Aquarius rose at the same time.

Antoninus Pius, who reigned between 138 and 161, and Marcus Aurelius (161-180), seem to have had few formal dealings with astrologers; at least, there is no record of any, and it has been conjectured that this was because of the increased influence of Stoic philosophy in Rome. If the future is absolutely fixed, then no amount of foreknowledge can make any difference; and in that case, what is the point of prediction?

As might be expected, however, Aurelius accepted astrology as a useful tool. He was interested too in dreams as a means of divination. He had the horoscopes of his twin sons drawn up, when they were born in August 161. Both were favourable, and the fact that the elder boy died when he was four does not seem to have shaken the Emperor's faith. He settled the succession on his younger son, Commodus.

As unattractive a personality as ever sat on the throne of Rome, Commodus' spare time was spent enjoying himself in tavern or brothel, or stripped naked to take part in gladiatorial combat in the public arena. He was as much star-worshipper as genuine astrologer, and saw astrology as some kind of superstitious quasi-religion rather than as a scientific system. His successor, Septimus Severus, returned to a more sensible, practical view. Born in Africa, he rose to high rank under Marcus Aurelius, and is known to have consulted an astrologer about his own destiny. His promotion to the tribunate in 176 confirmed that good fortune was accurately foretold. During a brief eclipse from favour under Commodus, he advertised for a marriageable woman whose horoscope should conform to his own, and found one in a Syrian, H. Julia Donna, who bore him two sons, one of whom was nicknamed Caracalla.

Severus was unwise enough, when praetorian governor of Sicily, to be discovered once more consulting an astrologer about his 'imperial destiny', as Cassius Dio put it. But (because, the historian suggested, Commodus was so cordially detested) the local authorities did not prosecute him; indeed, they crucified the unfortunate man unwise enough to have betrayed him!

After the death of Commodus and a short period of struggle for the throne, Severus occupied it, supported in his bid for power by the prognostications of several astrologers and by other miscellaneous divinations. Decorating his new imperial palace, he had his horoscope painted on the ceilings of the rooms in which he held court - although not in such detail as to give away to the casual observer the precise moment of his birth, so the horoscope could be used against him.

Severus seems to have been almost manic in his acceptance of any astrological prediction made with sufficient assurance, although the stoical attitude of some of his predecessors was entirely absent in him, and he evidently believed that if he intervened with determination in the planetary plan, he could depend on some mitigation of astrological prophesy. For instance, he executed numerous people – including several of his friends – on the grounds that they had consulted astrologers to discover the best time at which to assassinate him.

Severus is said to have left Rome for Britain in the knowledge that he would not survive the campaign there. Caracalla, having murdered his younger brother Geta, for safety's sake, seems to have had the same total belief in astrology as his father. Astrologer after astrologer was summoned to advise him, and several of them – an Egyptian called Serapio, one called Ascletion, and Larginus Proculus—told the Emperor that he would not live long, and that his successor would be Macrinus, a prefect. Ascletion was executed, Larginus Proculus was promised execution immediately after the date on which he had said Caracalla would die, and Serapio was thrown to a lion (which simply licked his hand, so a more prosaic execution had to be arranged).

Nevertheless, Caracalla was murdered, and for the next several decades astrology took a less prominent part in imperial manœuvrings. Neither Opellus Macrinus, who reigned only for a year, nor Elagabalus, a demented young man who took the name of his Sun god and was slaughtered when he was 18 by his praetorian guard, contributed anything to its history; and Severus Alexander, who reigned between 222 and 235, was said to be an astrologer but did not use the skill ostentatiously.

What he did do was encourage professional astrologers to organize themselves into a body that could pass on knowledge in a proper manner, actually advertising themselves as teachers; and he seems to have seen to it, too, that astrology was given precedence when the curriculum at the Athenaeum in Rome, founded by Hadrian, was reorganized.

As the power and influence of Rome passed its apogee, Christianity began to increase its hold, and eventually under Constantine in 334 was to be proclaimed as the official state religion, thus doing astrology the enormous service of reducing it from the status of a religious and magical art to that of a science. What, during these first centuries AD, was the state of the theory and literature of the subject?

The *Tetrabiblos* has already been mentioned as probably the most distinguished of astrological textbooks. The *Anthologiae* of Vettius Valens was enormously popular, perhaps because whereas Ptolemy wrote substantially for the educated layman and explored the subject scientifically, Valens was himself an astrologer, and intended his work for believers.

We know little of the life of Vettius Valens, except that he never grew rich, was never involved in politics or fashion and so, avoiding execution for favouring this imperial candidate or that, remained relatively unknown. He seems to have bolstered his income by running, for a time, a school of astrology (he dedicated his book to one of his students, Marcus). It is impossible to reconstitute the *Anthologiae*, which was in nine books; but it was to be used by generations of astrologers up until the 8th century at least, when Theophilus was still quoting it.

Some popular astrological writing was in verse: among the astrological versifiers were Astrampsychus, Dorotheus of Sidon, and Manetho. Astrampsychus left a hundred and one astrological aphorisms, printed in alphabetical order. Anubio, who may have been an Egyptian, left work which was to be used by Firmicus Magnus, Hephaestion, Palchrus and Rhetorius, over the next four centuries. Dorotheus, an Arab, left his *Pentateuch*, five books, dealing with births, eras of time, the Lords of the Horoscope, the computation of birth years, and 'undertaking' or the divination of events in a life. And to the professional astrologers must be added those who believed astrology to be an important part of their studies, like the physicians Antigonus of Nicaea and Galen.

Medical astrology was already beginning to rationalize its beliefs. These were never fatalistic; after all, if fate determined whether or not a patient should recover from or succumb to an illness, what point would there be in treating him? Galen (130–*c* 200) studied medicine at Pergamos, where he was born, then in Corinth and Alexandria, and finally in Rome (where he became physician to Marcus Aurelius, and later attended Commodus and Severus). He was careful always to note the precise time at which a patient had taken to bed with an illness; carefully considered the position of Sirius, the dog star, when medicine was being prepared or administered; insisted that the *theriac*, a medicine which he had developed, should be taken at the third hour of the first or fourth day of the Moon; and in one of his medical treatises devoted twelve chapters to the influence of the Moon in each of the zodiac signs, also dealing with the positions of the planets. Antigonus went further, publishing a collection of 'medical horoscopes' which doctors used for at least two centuries to help them in treating patients.

Not a single writer, as far as can be discovered, argued that the planets could have no influence on human affairs, although there were many arguments about the degree to which they enabled a practitioner to predict events, or delineate character. The most distinguished of the 'opponents'

A coin of Perinthus or Heracleia, one of many bearing either one sign of the Zodiac or (as here) all of them, set around the outside edge

of astrology, or those who believed that astrologers' powers of divination were extremely limited, was Plutarch (c 46-120), a journalist who wrote on philosophy, morals and, of course, biography. He never organized or even rationalized his objections to astrology, simply pointing out that man had a very generous capacity for accepting anything 'magical', and arguing strongly against the conception of an immutable Fate.

He had little effect on the faithful. In the 2nd century came a more considerable antagonist of fatalistic astrology, Favorinus of Arles, who seems to have had many an argument on the subject with the Emperor Hadrian, who was of course of a very different persuasion. Favorinus' arguments were not always very well-founded: for instance, he believed that astrology was a new fad, and that astrologers had invented the so-called ancients who they claimed had founded the art. He then (and this argument is reiterated to this day) claimed that all astrological predictions were so general as to be meaningless; went on to say that anyway, man's time on earth was far too brief for him to be able to fathom such a complicated theory; asked how astrology could be used to forecast the weather when good and bad weather existed at the same time in different places; demanded to know why the time of birth under one constellation should be considered when the time of conception under another was ignored (a good point); doubted whether the precise moment of birth could ever be discovered; and – another appealing point – asked whether it was not ridiculous and unbearable to suggest that all our actions, down to deciding whether or not to take a bath, were predestined.

Ptolemy disposes of most of these criticisms. But in any case opposition was not (any more than defence) on rational grounds. Someone who heard Favorinus give an anti-astrological lecture described how he summed up:

Astrologers predict either adverse or propitious events. If they foretell prosperity and deceive you, you will be made wretched by vain expectations; if they foretell adversity, you will be made wretched by useless fears ... The anticipation of your hopes will wear you out with suspense. Therefore there is every reason why you should not resort to men of that kind who profess knowledge of the future.

One of the ironies of Roman astrological history is that so many emperors who almost uncritically accepted the influence of the planets patronized scholars who argued against it. Favorinus had argued with Hadrian; Septimus Severus, almost fanatically attached to the most fatalistic aspects of astrology, appointed Alexander of Aphrodisias to the chair of the Peripatetic School at Athens, from where he issued his essay *On Fate*, in which he denied that the planets could affect human destiny – though even he agreed that they must influence non-human aspects of life on earth, such as the elements, 'the creation, destruction, and in general all transformation of matter. They also determine all terrestrial motion.'

Astrology was included in the multifarious criticisms levelled at almost all human knowledge by Sextus Empiricus, the Greek physician and sceptic philosopher, who in the late 2nd and early 3rd centuries attacked literature and philology, rhetoric, geometry, arithmetic ('number is nothing'), music, logic and physics. Even he excepted astrological meteorology from his general condemnation, but as for individual horoscopes – they were nonsense! He summarized astrological knowledge as it was known in his time, and then demolished each point in turn – or attempted to. Some of his criticisms are entirely valid (the difficulty of knowing the precise birth time, for instance); others were based on misunderstandings (which seem, sometimes, almost contrived); and others were simply vapid. He asks for instance why 'someone born under Leo should be strong and brave just because that constellation is called Leo', or why someone born under Virgo should be considered likely to be fair while an Ethiopian born under the same sign would undoubtedly be swarthy. Silly sooth.

Sextus Empiricus' only really rational criticism, and one for which there was much to be said, was that there was just not enough scientific data known to astrologers to enable them to present their science *as* a science. But nevertheless, his arguments against astrology were to appeal to a band of people whose attitude to the subject, if often confused, was to affect its history for a thousand years and more. The Greek satirist Lucian, whose own attack on astrology lacked muscle, lashed out in his abhorrence of the subject at a relatively new cult, a gang of simple-minded followers of a crucified sophist, one Jesus Christ. The 'Christians' approached astrology with almost superstitious caution.

VI

THE COMING OF
CHRISTIANITY

ALMOST the first story we hear about the birth of Jesus is of the 'wise men from the east' who came to Herod to announce that they knew that the King of the Jews had been born because they had 'seen his star in the east'. Herod, having 'enquired of them diligently what time the star appeared' sent them out to Bethlehem to seek for the child, 'and lo, the star, which they saw in the east, went before them, till it came and stood over where the young child was.'

There has been much speculation about what 'the star' was: general opinion suggests it may have been a conjunction of Jupiter and Saturn, possibly with Uranus, which would have made for a very bright and apparently single 'star' moving quickly enough to fulfil the conditions of the story. But that is astronomical speculation. The significance of the story for us is that it shows how, right at the beginning of the accounts of Christ's life, astrology played a part.

It would have been remarkable had it been otherwise. To most thoughtful men of the time there would have been no question of a god being born without the fact being announced in the heavens, probably by some strange but obvious celestial phenomenon rather than by his having a remarkable personal horoscope. Apart from the truth or otherwise of the story, it was to say the least extremely helpful to those set on establishing the divinity of Christ to have his birth associated with a spectacular astrological event; no scientist of the time would have accepted the possibility of such a phenomenon unless astrological observation supported it. In fact, of course, the appearance of a single rogue star has no astrological significance, and had none at the time; but the problem of inventing a significant horoscope for a divinity by choosing a propitious moment for the birth boggles the astrological mind, and was certainly beyond the early Christians, if the idea indeed ever occurred to them. The next best thing was some kind of spectacular 'comet-like' event, which was what is said to have occurred.

The presence in St Matthew's Gospel of the 'three wise men', or kings, or Magi, or astrologers, was to be rather an embarrassment to some of the fathers of the Church; later generations were simply to deny that they were astrologers at all, although that was clearly what the author of the gospel intended. The earliest commentator to seize the nettle and attack the myth was St John Chrysostom (c 347–407), who made heavy weather of his criticism, not so much attacking the notion of astrology itself as berating the three astrologers for calling Jesus the King of the Jews when 'his kingdom was not of this world', and suggesting that they were unwise to the point of foolishness in coming to Bethlehem, stirring things up with the king, and instantly leaving. He also pointed out (quite rightly) that the appearance of a single star was not in accordance with astrological tradition, although he agreed that its appearance was a sign that God favoured the wise men. Tacitly, he admitted that he not only believed in the appearance of the star, but that it was shown to the astrologers for a purpose, so demolishing his own argument.

Speculation about the wise men was to continue for centuries, with various embroideries. There were not always three, for instance; Chrysostom suggested that there may have been a dozen, and in the earliest Christian art other numbers are given. The Magi do not seem to have been promoted to royal status until as late as the 6th century, and the Venerable Bede, the English historian of the 7th century, seems to be the first man to give their names. Their original home was in Arabia, or Persia, or Chaldea, or India, according to which early authority one reads, and anyone interested in visiting their tomb should look in Cologne, for after their deaths the Empress Helena brought their bodies from India to Constantinople, whence they travelled to Milan and on to Germany.

Some Christian commentators invested them with various magical powers, perhaps to denigrate them, and thereby astrology in general; a 10th-century dramatist tells how they flew miraculously to Bethlehem after the birth, causing considerable surprise to the citizens of the cities over which they passed. But some sects seized on the story as proof of astrology as God's means of regulating affairs on earth. A heretical sect, the Priscillianists, did so, prompting a 10th-century writer to put forward all the traditional anti-astrological arguments, and to present the 'wise men' simply as the first Gentiles to seek Christ.

Christian opposition to astrology from earliest times to our own has been founded in temperament rather than theology. No considerable Christian scholar or theologian has argued that astrology is unthinkable, except when or if it claims to predict the future, and therefore contests the doctrine of free will. Many of the earliest authorities have astrological allusions. The Old Testament figure Enoch, for instance, claimed to be sixth in descent from Adam and Eve, has passages on the stars and herbs, gems and numbers, and claims that in the sixth heaven angels attend the phases of the Moon and the revolutions of stars and Sun, superintending the good or evil condition of the world. Enoch's notions of angels are somewhat eccentric (some of them have 'privy members like those of horses'), but it seems that two hundred of them so fancied earthly women that they came to live on earth, and betrayed to man various secrets, including the science of astrology, magic, witchcraft and divination, and the art of 'writing with ink and paper'.

Philo Judaeus, who lived in Alexandria soon after the death of Christ, hotly denied that the planets absolutely ruled men's lives, attacking astrologers who claimed that the whole of life was subject to the movements of the heavens. He did, however, believe the stars to be beautiful divine beings, intelligent animals who, unlike man, were incapable of evil. He believed also, indeed 'knew', that it was possible to predict 'disturbances and commotions of the earth from the revolutions of the heavenly bodies, and innumerable other events which have turned out most exactly true.'

A Syrian missionary called Bardesanes (154-222) has left in *The Dialogue Concerning Fate* a good account of what seems to be the most general early Christian attitude to astrology. It was evidently important to tackle the very strong public commitment to the subject, the result of centuries during which its truths had on the whole been accepted as self-evident. Bardesanes takes the pragmatic view: that it is obvious that there is some force from the planets, but this was given them by God and is therefore subject to His will, limited by Him through subjection to free will on the one hand and other natural forces on the other.

The Gnostics, an oriental religious movement which played a part in early Christianity, spawning many sects, believed (according to one text) that when Jesus ascended into heaven after the crucifixion, he changed the influences and even the movements of the planets (among other things making them turn to the right for six months of the year, whereas previously they had faced left), and determined how they shaped a new soul, controlled the process of conception and the formation of the embryo in the womb, and every event of life from cradle to tomb. (Incidentally, it is interesting that in the Arabic *Gospel of the Infancy*, attributed to St James, Jesus is an astronomer, lecturing the priests in the temple on 'the number of the spheres and heavenly bodies, as also their triangular, square and sextile aspect; their progressive and retrograde motion; their twenty-fourths and sixtieths of the twenty-fourths and other things which the reason of man had never discovered . . .')

Many Christian thinkers saw astrology as a demonstration of the universe devised by God. *The Recognitions*, an anthology of letters allegedly written to James, Jesus' brother, by Clement of Rome, a friend and confidant of St Peter, represents the planets and stars as fixed in heaven by God in order that 'they might be for an indication of things past, present and future', although only to be understood by the learned who had studied the subject in depth. Abraham was one of these; being an astrologer, he 'was able from the rational system of the stars to recognize the Creator, while all other men were in error, and understand that all things are regulated by his Providence.'

Clement charmingly called the twelve Apostles the Twelve Months of Christ, who himself was the Year of our Lord. The planets are admitted to have an evil as well as a good influence; 'possessing freedom of the will, we sometimes resist our desires and sometimes yield to them'. Arguments against astrology are restricted to resisting the idea that there is no Providence and that everything happens by chance and *genesis*, that 'whatever your *genesis* contains, that shall befall you'. It is unthinkable that God should make man sin through an evil disposition of the planets, and then punish him for it! It is also pointed out – and later astrologers have often repeated this, both as explanation and excuse – that the movements and inter-relationships of the planets are so complex, and understanding and interpreting them so difficult, that no astrologer is to be blamed for misreading them.

The argument between Origen, an orthodox Christian who lived between 185 and 253, and the philosopher Celsus, who in 176-80 produced *The True Word*, an anti-Christian tract, inevitably involved astrology. Celsus took the view that the main idiocy of many practised by Christians was the denial of the power of the planets; Origen asserted that the whole idea of free will was demolished if one accepted that the stars were rational beings, and assigned by God to the nations on earth. He accepted that the planets' movements could foretell events, and was particularly attached to the idea of comets as omens, which had announced wars and natural disasters, but also the birth of Christ.

Tertullian, born in about 160, and an eloquent early writer about Christianity, argued that it was the fallen angels who had taught man astrology (and, incidentally, metallurgy and botany). These angels, who lived in the clouds conveniently near the stars, were inevitably excellent meteorologists. Nevertheless, Christians would do well to reject them and their notions, despite the fact that the Magi were astrologers. He obviously saw it as extremely worrying that 'astrology nowadays, forsooth, treats of Christ; is the science of the stars of Christ, not of Saturn and Mars', and argues that since the coming of Christ the drawing up of horoscopes should be discontinued. He was especially pleased that at the time of writing astrologers were positively forbidden to enter Rome.

Many Christian apologists made it their business to read the published works of astrologers, in order to refute them; others took the short cut of simply reading anti-astrological works and repeating their arguments. Hippolytus, for instance, who lived in Italy and wrote in Greek (he was buried in Rome in 236) lifted his arguments straight from the writings of Sextus Empiricus.

The most prominent of all early antagonists of astrology, St Augustine, cannot entirely be freed from the accusation of taking a short cut, or at least not thinking the subject through thoroughly or originally. Augustine was born in 345 (he died in 430) in Numidia, of a devoutly Christian mother. A trained rhetorician, he was at first a Manichean, but was converted to Christianity by the sermons of Ambrose, Bishop of Milan, where Augustine was teaching rhetoric. His early life, which included various sexual irregularities, is frankly described in his *Confessions*, and astrology is mentioned there too; but his main attack on it comes in the *Christian Doctrine* and *The City of God*.

His case against astrology is simple, unsubtle and mistaken: simply that it enslaves human will by claiming that the entire course of a life can be predicted from the stars. If predictions did come true, he said, it was through coincidence or demonic intervention. 'Those that hold', he writes in the fifth book of *The City of God*,

that the stars do manage our action, our passions, good or ill, without God's appointment, are to be silenced and not to be heard, be they of the true religion or be they bondslaves to idolatry of what sort soever; for what does this opinion do but flatly exclude all deity? ... and what part has God left him in thus disposing of human affairs, if they be swayed by a necessity from the stars, whereas He is Lord of stars and men.

He then produced the old argument that if astrology worked, twins should have precisely the same destiny. (If they did, incidentally, it was

nothing to do with astrology, he said, but because their background, environment, upbringing was similar; if they did not, it was a proof that astrology did not work.) True, Nigidius had tried to explain the dissimilarity between the lives of twins by rapidly turning a pot on a potter's wheel and splashing ink upon it, showing how far apart the splashes landed, and adducing from this that on a swiftly turning earth the planets would be in different positions even for twins born with one holding the other's heel. St Augustine was unimpressed. If astrology was as complicated as that, how could an astrologer possibly claim to be able to make firm predictions? (He seems to have taken this, and several other arguments, more or less straight from Cicero's *De divinatione*.)

The trouble with Augustine's anti-astrological arguments is that they are founded (like those of so many other critics throughout history) on a misunderstanding of the nature of the astrological theory, even as it was practised in his own time. Very few astrologers argued that the planets absolutely controlled every aspect of the life of man, much less that every living thing was under a similar governance. When he points out that astrology is ridiculous because a cow and a human baby born at the same instant do not have precisely the same life, he simply displays his own ignorance of what astrology claims, and his stronger arguments are proportionally weakened. His supposition that astrologers claim that the time and place of birth *and nothing else* control a man's destiny leads him to concentrate on that point to the exclusion of more eccentric claims which would have offered him a wider target. He seems to have read very little astrological literature (not, for instance, the *Tetrabiblos*, which might be thought required reading for anyone preparing an attack on astrology).

St Augustine is still often set up as the prime Christian opponent of astrology; and so he is. But that is not saying much. Even he admits that the Sun and planets have an effect on some material things such as the tides, and hence on some living things such as shellfish. It might be argued that he performed a considerable service to astrology by attacking its occult aspects, while not condemning out of hand the kind of scientific astrology that was to provide the more rewarding areas of experiment in the future.

The City of God is seen as the apogee of Christianity's attacks on astrology, and so in a sense it was. That it is an unintelligent, derivative and ineffectual attack is neither here nor there; happily, the Christian church's generally antagonistic view of science in general has in the long run been equally ineffectual. When Augustine argued that 'Christians have many better and more serious things to occupy their time than such

OPPOSITE
St Augustine's *Confessions* revealed that he once had an enthusiastic belief in astrology. Later, he was convinced that the theory was fallacious, although the arguments he advances against it are mostly based on misunderstandings and false premises, drawn from earlier critics

subtle investigations concerning the relative magnitude of the stars and the intervals of space between them', he was setting the tone for the official Church attitude to science for many centuries. It has not, in the end, prevailed, even in schools.

The fact that some Christian astrologers were not deterred is illustrated by the work of Julius Firmicus Maternus, a contemporary who is likely to have read Augustine. His *Matheseos* of *c* 354 accepted the doctrine of free will, but found it odd that man should think the stars and planets mere decoration of the heavens.

Firmicus, whose mind seems to have been a great deal keener than Augustine's (if we are to judge from the organization of his book and the deployment of his arguments), produced one by one the chief anti-astrological arguments and demolished them with ease, demonstrating clearly that the critics had not for the most part bothered to understand the subject. He admits that some astrologers are rogues and others fools, he admits the difficulty of the subject – but claims that the human spirit is capable of coping with it, as it is capable of coping with the mapping of the heavens and the prediction of the planets' courses.

In a brilliantly presented and enormously complex argument, Firmicus in the second half of *Matheseos* scathingly demolishes superstition and its practitioners, the 'magicians' who 'stay in temples in an unkempt state and always walk abroad thus' in order to frighten people. While he accepts that 'magic' is a powerful force, he is violently opposed to secrecy in regard to it, and demands that astrologers, rather than shrinking from public view as though ashamed, should place themselves under the protection of God, praying that He should grant them 'grace to attempt the explanation of the courses of the stars'.

Matheseos was an important book, a major work that accurately and persuasively quoted earlier sources, and was itself to be quoted for centuries by Christian astrologers and theologians who wished to assuage the fears of laymen at times when the Church seemed to be condemning the practice.

OPPOSITE LEFT The association of parts of the human body with the signs of the zodiac was an early element of astrological medicine. A 15th-century 'astro-logical man' from the Guild Book of the Barber Surgeons of York is shown standing on the sign of Pisces, the fish (associated with the feet), and with Aries, the ram, crouching on his head

OPPOSITE RIGHT Christian antagonism to astrology was slow to develop – there is no direct attack in the Bible, for instance; provided that no claim was made to be able to foretell the future, there was no reason (it was argued) why God should not preside over a wholly Christian zodiac

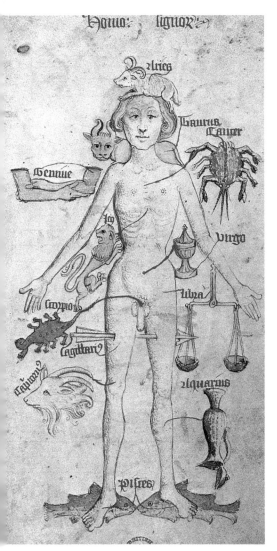

aries

taurus Cauer

Gemini

leo

scorpio

Cagittari?

Capiou

virgo

libra

aquarius

pisces

Sctm philosophoz deliram̄
notant̄ duo decisignata
abaricie in cipiam.

154

heco ma signa sunt corpo
ris hois. & signas solis ince
lo apparenus.

VII

ASTROLOGY IN MEDIEVAL EUROPE

THE early Middle Ages, while it produced a fair amount of argument about astrology, and saw a diminution of its influence on monarchs, did not mark as complete a collapse as some historians have suggested. Even where there was some doubt about its use on a personal level, it was still generally admitted to be useful in meteorology and agriculture. And most scholars took the view that it was an important element of general knowledge. Boethius, the 6th-century consul in Rome, some of whose writings were translated by King Alfred the Great, was one of them, and his book *The Consolation of Philosophy* must have been influential in reinforcing whatever knowledge of astrology there was in Britain in the 10th century. He argued that the movements of the planets derived from the immortal will of Providence, and that 'the celestial movement of the stars' translated that will into earthly events, 'constraining human forces in an indissoluble chain of causes which, since it starts from the decree of immovable Providence, must needs itself also be immutable.'

Nevertheless, he was not a fatalist, for even divine Providence imposed no fatal necessity on the human will, which was always free, while nature was not, but was constrained by the planets. As Canute found, you cannot argue with the tides. Boethius also, by the way, agreed with Plato that each planet has its own musical chord, contributing to the heavenly harmony of the music of the spheres.

An attraction of the astrological theory, in the early Middle Ages as now, was that it could be applied to absolutely every facet of human life.

But there were some areas into which it soaked with persuasive power, and among these was medicine. The 'astrological man' (see p 120) appears again and again in manuscripts of the period, though sometimes to denigrate astrology. There is for instance a splendid 11th-century drawing of the twelve signs grouped around the figure of Christ, hand raised to bless. The names of the parts of the body 'ruled' by the various signs appear – but the caption reads: 'According to the ravings of the philosophers the signs are thus denoted'!

Astrology was by now so integral a part of medicine that it was not to be possible to disentangle the two for many centuries. Until the 18th century it was still impossible to qualify as a doctor at some universities unless you had passed an examination in astrology, and the use of the planetary positions in diagnosis and treatment was a commonplace.

Like other theories, this was used to a greater or lesser degree according to the temperament of the physician. Constantinus Africanus, for instance, who lived between 1015 and 1087, was enormously important in the history of medicine mainly because of his translation and presentation of earlier medical textbooks. He had studied with Chaldeans, Arabs, Persians and Saracens as well as in Tunis (where he was born) and Baghdad. But in his *De humana natura*, apart from tracing the formation of the embryo in the womb and relating this to the positions of the planets, and including a certain amount of mildly eccentric material (someone who consistently wets the bed, for instance, should eat the bladder of a river fish for eight days while the Moon waxes and wanes), he makes relatively little of astrological medicine, though there can be no doubt he studied it.

It is not surprising that Constantinus studied in the East, for collaboration between Jewish and Arabian scholars had resulted in a correlation of astrological knowledge at such centres as Cairo, Baghdad, Alexandria and Kairwan in Tunis, which produced at least one remarkable scholar in Isaac ben Solomon Israeli, or Isaac Judaeus, who worked there in the 900s, and wrote books on medical astrology which survived for centuries (Robert Burton quotes from him in *The Anatomy of Melancholy*).

To trace the various contributions to what might be called 'Arabian' astrology is an almost impossibly complex task, for pieces of theory drifted towards the Arabian centres from as far away as China and India, as well as from Rome, Greece, Egypt and Persia. This was collected together in the great library founded in Baghdad by Harun al-Rashid and al-Mamun, caliphs of the Abbasside dynasty, and completed in about 850, where apart from the lesser works there were Greek copies of the *Tetrabiblos* translated for general use.

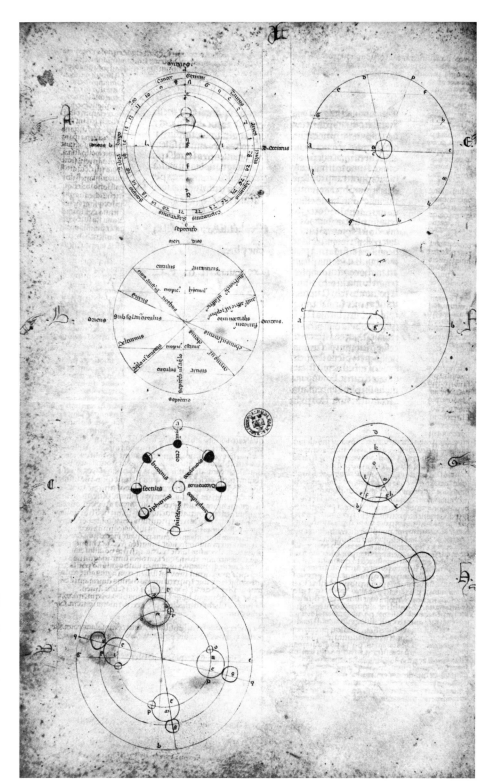

Boethius, a Roman philosopher and statesman, was the author of a substantial work on astronomy, and of *De Consolatione Philosophiae*, a dialogue between himself and philosophy; it has a highly religious, although non-Christian, tone, and astrology takes its place in the argument. Translations of the work were made into Anglo-Saxon by Alfred the Great and into English by Chaucer

There are hints of the importance of the work done in Baghdad in the writings, six or eight hundred years later, of some Englishmen. Chaucer, for instance, wrote a *Treatise on the Astrolabe* in the 14th century in which he made use of Messahala's *Commentary on Ptolemy*, written in the early 800s; William Lilly quotes from the same source in the 1640s; Dr Dee, in Elizabethan England, owned several manuscripts of Isaac Judaeus' works.

In other countries too the Arabian interest in astrology took hold; in Spain, for instance, where the Western Caliph founded in 948 an academy at Cordova at which Moors and Jews alike built up a body of knowledge which in its turn was disseminated through academies founded at Toledo and Granada. There, Hasdai ibn-Shaprut, a Jew, taught at the end of the 10th century, among other things rationalizing the assignation of all known herbs to separate planets which influenced their growth and virtue. Gerbert of Auvergne probably studied under him before being made Archbishop of Ravenna in 998, and later Pope, as Sylvester II. So there is evidence that Christians as well as Moors and Jews studied under Arabian auspices. Sylvester II was admittedly later accused of having had dealings with the Devil because of his studies at Cordova, and some Christians attempted to attach dark satanic inferences to anyone who had studied astrology; but progress was not, at this stage, to be denied.

Despite the vicissitudes of history – the capture of the Moorish cities of Spain by the Christians in the 11th century, for instance, and the

Aquarius and Pisces from the temple of Tiberius at Hamat, dated between the 3rd and 5th centuries AD

Astrolabes were used by astronomers to take the altitude of heavenly bodies – used, too, by travellers for making astronomical and topographical calculations. This, the earliest dated astrolabe, was made by Ahmad and Malmud in AD 984, and is in the Museum of the History of Science at Oxford

driving out of the Jews – the 'universities' at such cities as Toledo continued to function for centuries, with a continual stream of scholars benefiting from their libraries and their tradition of scholarship, all of which unhesitatingly supported astrology as a serious study.

From the 9th and 10th centuries, visual reminders have survived that help demonstrate the subject's fascination – sometimes illustrating slight differences between eastern and western astrology. In Islamic countries, human beings could not be represented by artists, and so the 'human' zodiac signs were altered: in place of the Geminian twins, Muslim artists showed two peacocks; a wheatsheaf replaced the girl in Virgo, and Aquarius became a mule carrying two baskets.

There is at Florence a splendid example of another work of art, this time with a practical purpose: an astrolabe for the latitude of Rome, said to have belonged to Sylvester II. An equally early one is at Oxford, made in 984 by Ahmad and Malmud, sons of Ibrahim, of Ispahan. The development of the astrolabe began, it is believed, in the 1st century BC – there are claims for it as the oldest scientific instrument. Used for measuring the altitude of the stars, it was essential to the astronomer-astrologer, and there are many fine examples of astrolabes in museums. It was often magnificently decorated, a pleasure to look at as well as to use.

The spread of astrology across Europe, the extent to which it was practised in any western country before the growth of the Roman Empire, is a subject that must be treated with the utmost delicacy. It depends to some extent, of course, on what kind of astrology one is talking about. It seems fairly clear that natal astrology, the setting up of a map of the sky for the moment of a birth, the construction and interpretation of a horoscope, was not possible in, say, Germany, France or Britain until well into the time of Imperial Rome; and that if it was possible then, the means were only known to a very few people, and those probably attached to Roman armies as Balbillus had been attached to Claudius' entourage during his journey to Britain.

However, if we accept that an interest in astrology often arose from a preoccupation with the simple observation of planetary movements, then the most primitive civilizations showed it, and it may be said that Stonehenge - for instance - betrays such a preoccupation, if we are to accept that that monument (and others like it) was erected to fulfil some astronomical purpose.

The many theories about the planning and erection of Stonehenge are too complex to investigate here; but the theory that it was some kind of astronomical computer, while suspect in some quarters, is quite sufficiently well argued to remain a possibility. Whatever its purpose, there certainly seems to be an astronomical connection; and the influence on an ignorant community (we are speaking of something like 2900 BC) of a priestly aristocracy that could forecast even the most basic solar and lunar events would have been very considerable. It is even suggested that the people of Neolithic Britain were ruled by such an aristocracy, the leaders of which possessed at least some of the knowledge of the early Babylonian astronomers. Much of their power as leaders of society may have been derived from their knowledge of astronomy, used 'magically' to invoke the aid of those heavenly gods, the planets, in hunting: a sort of astrology, although at that stage invoking the occult as intensely as - if much more vaguely than - the Babylonians or Egyptians did.

Three thousand years later we glimpse a more sophisticated astrology in the British Isles: although still much too dimly to draw detailed conclusions. The Druids remain sufficiently mysterious to enable the inventive to saddle them with all sorts of preoccupations of which they may have known nothing. Caesar recorded that the Druids in Gaul were men of dignity, lawgivers and priests, learned in astrology and the natural sciences. Britain seemed to be the headquarters of the Druid cult, if that is what it was, and there was an annual meeting in Gaul from which the most promising novices travelled to Britain for training, where they seem to have studied not only astrology but the same systems of divination as the Babylonians – using patterns of bird flight, for instance, and the convulsions of dying men.

Early Christian literature provides examples of the Druids predicting a child's future from the date of its birth, and the word for cloud divination (*neladóracht*) is also freely used to mean astrology and divination in general. There are several references to astrology itself; for instance, it is related how an astrologer calculated the planets' positions in order to tell the foster-father of St Columkille, better known as St Columba of Ireland, when it was a propitious time for the boy to begin lessons. It is clear too that the Druids operated a system of lucky and unlucky days: the thirteenth day of a lunar cycle was considered a bad one on which to begin anything; a boy born on that day would be 'courageous, bold, rapacious, arrogant, self-pleasing', and a girl 'saucy, spirited, and daring of her body with many men'.

Little is known about the patterns of international travel in ancient times; however, it is by no means impossible that, as some scholars have suggested, astronomical knowledge of all sorts reached Britain and western Europe in the earliest years of Babylon; it does not seem very likely that men should otherwise spontaneously have started building stone circles and similar monuments in various parts of the western world at the same time. Such legends as those that support the coming of Mediterranean traders to Britain many centuries before Christ may be far from nonsense; and while it does not seem at all likely that men with the knowledge to design and build such a sophisticated monument as Stonehenge would be travelling on a trader's boat, there is nothing inherently absurd in the idea: scholars have often also been adventurers.

We begin to see our way rather more clearly round about the time of the Roman occupation, when Mithraism brought knowledge of the existence of astrology to Gaul, Germany and Britain, and temples to the Roman gods were built – often on the sites of Druidic temples, it seems, for Caesar says that the Gauls worshipped Mercury, Apollo, Mars and Minerva (and can only have meant that they worshipped local gods *like* those Roman ones).

With the departure of the Roman legions, and the Dark Ages, astrology like so much else vanishes from our view, except for some hints that the knowledge brought by the Romans was treasured by some scholars, especially in the north and west of the province – at the limits of Roman

power, whence, eventually, came so many early scholars – Alcuin and
Bede, Adelard and Roger Bacon among them. Did the British who had
learned to read continue to treasure Roman books after AD 410? A few
relics suggest the answer – books in Greek or Latin with scribbled
comments and notes in a Scottish or Welsh dialect.

Geoffrey of Monmouth (c 1100–1154), that early romancer and historian, claims that in King Arthur's reign, whenever that may have been,

there subsisted at Carleon in Glamorganshire a college of two hundred philosophers, who studied astronomy and other sciences; and who were particularly
employed in watching the course of the stars, and predicting events to the king
from these observations.

By the time Geoffrey was writing, Christianity had long been established
in Britain; but as we have seen, this may well have meant increased
knowledge and approval of astrology rather than the reverse.

Can Geoffrey's word be accepted, though? Well, he tells us that his
Historia regum Britanniae is a translation of 'a certain very ancient book
written in the British language' (that is, Welsh) by Walter, Archdeacon
of Oxford. This may have been a simple, individual manuscript; in any
event, it has completely vanished. Geoffrey may have invented some of
his history, but he would not have invented it all – indeed his often
garbled records of some events match with those of which we have
knowledge, and he (or his original source) refers often to Cicero, Juvenal,
Lucan, Apuleius and others. So the evidence that astrology was in use 'at
the time of King Arthur' is worth something, if perhaps not a great deal.

Strands of astrological belief must have been preserved not only by the
faint and fading tenets of whatever 'religion' had been supported by the
Druids, but in the fading memories of Mithraism, if these communicated
themselves to the British, and in the heritage of knowledge left by Rome;
and Christianity contributed, too. In *The Panegyric of Lludd the Great*,
a poem written in the 6th century by Taliesin, the 'mythical' British bard,
there is a passage, among many dealing with prophesies, which reads

> To Britain shall come an exaltation,
> Britons of the stock of Rome,
> May I be judged by the merciful God.
>
> Astronomers are predicting
> Misfortune in the land.
>
> Druids are prophesying
> Beyond the sea, beyond Britain,
> That the summer shall not be fair . . .

Of little value except as evidence, again, that some knowledge of astrology persevered. The *Anglo-Saxon Chronicle* agrees. This was written at various centres up to the mid-12th century; the earlier parts probably originated with King Alfred (871–900). It records various eclipses, and other planetary phenomena. (It also, incidentally, records the travels of the 'three astrologers' – rather than kings or wise men – to Christ's birthplace.) The *Chronicle* mostly interprets eclipses and comets as symbols of foreboding. In 664, we are told, an eclipse on 10 May brought not only the death of the King of Kent, but a plague; fourteen years later, a comet in August presaged Bishop Wilfrid's expulsion from his bishopric. The comet of 729 brought a clutch of disasters: St Egbert died, and the Atheling Osward, and Osric, King of Northumbria.

Among the astronomical reports appear records of more astonishing incidents: a number of fiery dragons flew over Northumbria in 793 (possibly the Leonide meteors); in 979 'was seen a bloody welkin oft times in likeness of a fire'. But for the most part the authors concentrate on comets and eclipses – including the most famous comet of all, Halley's, which appeared in 1066, and is shown in the Bayeux Tapestry above the head of the crowned King William the Conqueror.

By the beginning of the 8th century, the names of individual astrologers begin to appear: such men as Aldhelm, who was taught at the school in Kent started by Abbot Hadrian and his friend Theodore, Archbishop of Canterbury – the latter came from Tarsus in Asia Minor, and the two men certainly taught in Greek as well as Latin. Aldhelm left treatises on astrology, as well as on logic and arithmetic, meant as textbooks for future students. Alcuin, or Ealhwine, was educated at York, at a school with a long history (it has been suggested that its tradition went back to the Roman occupation), and went on to become a friend and adviser of the Emperor Charlemagne. He learned, he said, among other things, 'the harmony of the sky', the laws governing the rising and setting of the stars and the seven planets.

Some of the art and architecture of Britain before the 11th century has astrological references – sometimes at a distance, as when we hear for instance that the old Abbey of Glastonbury had a zodiac in its floor. There is zodiacal ornamentation in a number of pre-Conquest churches in Kent, and the new Canterbury Cathedral had some zodiac figures in it simply because the old one, burned down in 1067, had had them. There are 8th-century zodiacal drawings among the Harleian manuscripts in the British Library, and when the Abbey of Croyland was burned in 1091, according to a history compiled from ancient manuscripts that survived the fire, we lost a most beautiful and precious table, fabricated of different kinds of metals, according to the variety of the stars and heavenly signs. Saturn was of copper, Jupiter of gold, Mars of iron, the Sun of lattern [a yellow metal like brass], Mercury of amber, Venus of tin, and the Moon of silver. The eyes were charmed, as well as the mind instructed, by beholding the coloured circles, with the Zodiac and all its signs formed with wonderful art of metals and precious stones, according to their several natures, forms, figures and colours.

After the Norman conquest a new flow of astrological material reached England with Jewish scholars from France and elsewhere who settled not only in London, Oxford and Cambridge, but in other large towns, bringing with them books which contained astrological lore, particularly from Arabic and Moorish sources. There is a tradition that William the Conqueror had his own astrologer, who set the time for his coronation (midday on Christmas Day, 1066) – and astrologers claim that this was a particularly auspicious moment, unlikely to have been chosen at random, and take it as the moment for which to set up a general 'horoscope' for England.

It was during William's reign that perhaps the most notable of 11th-century English scholars was born, at Bath. Much of the life of Adelard, or Æthelhard, is dark to us, although he certainly travelled extensively in Europe, and perhaps further afield, for in one of his books he says with authority that 'what the schools of Gaul do not know, those beyond the Alps reveal; what you do not learn among the Latins, well-informed Greece will teach you.' He is fond, too, of quoting from Arabic texts, and does so, often, as though he is using verbal rather than literary sources.

Among his works are many on mathematics, astronomy and alchemy. He seems to have been somewhat strait-laced, or at least to have found the atmosphere of England uncongenial after his travels to more refined lands, for on his return he finds the country under Henry I filled with villainous fellows:

Princes are violent, prelates wine-bibbers, judges mercenary, patrons inconstant, the common men flatterers, promise-makers false, friends envious, and everyone in general ambitious.

He intends, he says, to settle down to serious work, and certainly did so. He translated several Arabic astrological works, including some (the tables of al-Khowarizmi, for instance) which were directed at teaching the reader to set up a horoscope. He would scarcely have done this had he not been interested in the subject, or indeed had been unable himself to set up a chart. His view was that the planets were 'superior and divine animals' which were 'the causers and principle of inferior natures'. One who studied then could understand the present and the past and predict the future. His charming view of the stars as celestial pets extends to a consideration of their food, which he believed consisted of the humidities of earth and water, refined by a long journey through the upper air, and which by the time they reached the planets were sufficiently light and ethereal not to dull their wits or make them put on weight.

Another treatise which was probably written by Adelard quotes from Hermes Trismegistus, Ptolemy, Apollonius and other ancient authorities, and argues for the use of astrology in medicine, for its study makes for better doctors than 'the narrow medical man who thinks of no effects except those of inferior nature merely'. He also deals with the planets' effects on animals and plants, and ascribes to them certain metals and colours – and indeed religions: the Jews are ruled by Saturn, the Arabs by Mars and Venus, Christianity by the Sun and Jupiter (for the Sun stands for honesty, liberality and victory, and Jupiter for peace, equity and humanity). The continual battles between the Jews, the Muslims and the Christians are explained by the fact that neither Mars nor Saturn is ever in friendly relation with Jupiter.

More or less contemporary with Adelard was William of Conches. He also travelled extensively before becoming associated with the court of Geoffrey Plantagenet as tutor of his son, the future King Henry II of England, between 1146 and 1149. Interestingly, William is one of the first scholars to attempt a definition of the difference between astronomy and astrology. Authorities, he says, speak of the planets in three ways: the fabulous, the astrological and the astronomical. Those interested in fables interpret the Greek myths as if they were astronomical. The astrologers treat phenomena as they *appear* to be, whether accurately or no. Astronomers deal with things as they *are*, whether they seem to be so or not.

He takes the argument no further, but does not seem to be intending to denigrate astrology, for he goes on to misquote Plato in support of the theory that the planets control nature and the human body. The heavenly bodies, he argues, heat the atmosphere, which in turn heats water – which forms a fundamental part of all animal bodies – and so must affect every living thing. He lists the planets and their qualities and humours, and puts forward some theories about how the principles were discovered, not only suggesting practical but symbolic reasons. The ancients, he suggests, discovered that Saturn was a 'cold' planet because when the Sun was cooler than usual it was in Cancer and in conjunction with Saturn in the same sign. But he also pointed out that Saturn was said to carry a scythe because a man who did so 'did more execution when receding than advancing'. Venus was said to have committed adultery with Mars because when those two planets were close together, Mars took away some of Venus' good influences.

It has been suggested that Henry II's interest in astrology, fostered by his tutor William of Conches and by his father Geoffrey, Count of Anjou, was sufficient to make him the patron of Abenezra (1092-1167), a Jew from Toledo, who came to England in 1158 to lecture in London and Oxford. He was also a poet:

> The planets and stars in their courses
>   Made way when I first saw the light;
> If I were a seller of candles
>   The Sun it would shine all the night.
>
> I try to succeed, but I cannot,
>   For the heavenly spheres oppose;
> If I took to winding-sheet sewing,
>   Then no-one would die, I suppose.

Abenezra seems to have had a pleasant sense of humour as well as considerable fame as an astrologer-writer (his *De nativitatibus* was reprinted in the 15th and 16th centuries). He lectured not only in England but all over Europe, and may briefly have occupied the chair of astrology at the university of Bologna.

Both Adelard and William of Conches were important in bringing to France and England more Arabic works, some of which they translated, and some of which they used as source material for their own books. There were of course other translators, many of whose names have been lost, though we know others – Bartholomew of Messina, Burgundio of Pisa and Eugenius, Admiral of Sicily, who translated from the Greek; Egidius de Trebaldis of Parma, Arnold of Barcelona and Blasius Armegandus of Montpellier, who translated from the Arabic, and so on. Through their work a great stream of astrological knowledge from Arabia made its way westward – some translators, like Pedro Alfonso, claimed to be intent on bringing knowledge westward to save greater scholars than he the labour of travelling so far to acquire the basis on which they could construct their philosophies.

Most translators and scholars believed in observation and experiment as well as the acquisition of knowledge from books. Pedro believed strongly in experience as a good master: 'It has been proved by experimental argument', he says, 'that we can truly affirm that the Sun and Moon and other planets exert their influences in earthly affairs... And indeed many other innumerable things happen on earth in accordance with the courses of the stars, and pass unnoticed by the senses of most

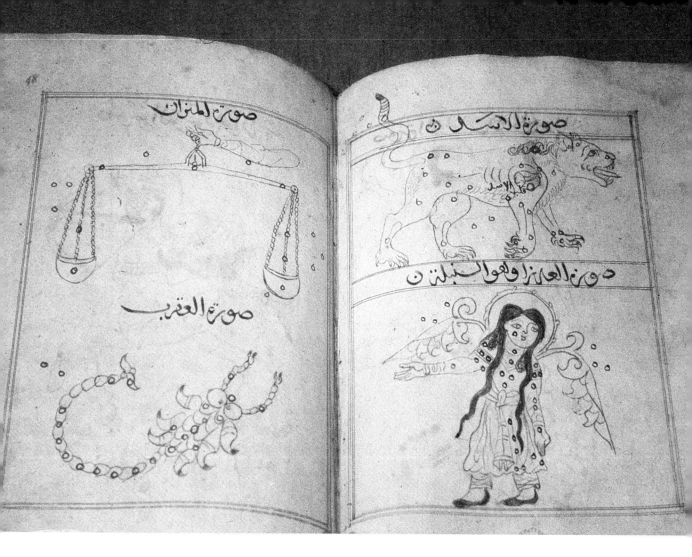

صورة الميزان

صورة العقرب

صورة الاسد

الاسد

دور العذرا والهوا السنبلة

Astrological works from the Middle East circulated freely in the West, and were immediately recognizable to western astrologers: this manuscript from 13th-century Turkey shows drawings of Leo, Libra and Scorpio symbols which differ not at all from the western representations; the Virgo, however, is unmistakably an eastern damsel

men, but are discovered and understood by the subtle acumen of learned men who are skilled in this art.' He was, incidentally, physician to King Henry I of England, and left notes on astrological medicine. Twenty years after his death, Walcher, Prior of Malvern, made translations of all Pedro's books into English.

It was during the 12th century that a great acceleration occurred in the translation of astrological texts into Latin. By 1150, most major texts were available in that language – Plato of Tivoli had translated the *Tetrabiblos* (as the *Quadripartitum*); John of Seville made a version of the *Centiloquium*, a series of astrological aphorisms attributed (wrongly) to Ptolemy, and translated Albumasar, Alchabitius and Messahala. And Gerard of Cromona (1114–87) made over seventy translations from the Arabic into the Latin, among them Ptolemy's *Almagest* (*Syntaxis*), and two previously unknown works of Aristotle, the *Meteorologica* and the *Generatione et corruptione*.

By the end of the first decade of the 13th century, the complete works
of Aristotle were for the first time available in Western Europe in a
language that every scholar could read, and by 1255, despite the misgiv-
ings of some churchmen, they were accepted in the universities. This was
a great step forward for astrology, for it meant that no serious theologian
would now contest the fact that the processes of change and growth on
earth depended on the activities of the heavenly bodies; read the medieval
scholars on Aristotle, and we find them all – from Albertus Magnus to
Thomas Aquinas and Dante – accepting the astrological theory which
had become a part of the philosopher's arguments; if they held strongly
to free will as a cornerstone of Christian teaching, they could not now
deny Aristotle's (or, for that matter, Augustine's) admission that the
planets influenced human affairs. The Church was forced to see astrology
as a science, and recognized it while at the same time condemning
magic. Thomas Aquinas is explicit in his *Summa theologiae:*

The majority of men ... are governed by their passions, which are dependent
upon bodily appetites; in these the influence of the stars is clearly felt. Few
indeed are the wise who are capable of resisting their animal instincts. Astrologers, consequently, are able to foretell the truth in the majority of cases,
especially when they undertake general predictions. In particular predictions,
they do not attain certainty, for nothing prevents a man from resisting the
dictates of his lower faculties. Wherefore the astrologers themselves are wont to
say that 'the wise man rules the stars' forasmuch, namely, as he rules his own
passions.

The spate of translations from the Arabic introduced a new element
into western astrology. Ptolemy in the *Tetrabiblos* had concerned himself
almost entirely with *judicial* astrology – using the positions of the planets
at the time of someone's birth to look at the child's future. He ignored
two aspects of astrology more important to the Arabs: *interrogationes*
and *electiones.* The first concerned itself with setting up a chart in order
to discover the answer to a question – the identity of a thief, perhaps, or
the nature of a proposed marriage. The second was a way of discovering
the propitious moment for a certain action – the sailing of a vessel, the
starting of a business, the consummation of a marriage.

The election of a particular moment of time was much used by doctors
to discover the proper moment at which to apply medicine, perform an
operation, raise a patient from bed; in a sense it is still used in the 20th
century when at least some doctors choose to operate at phases of the
moon when a patient is likely to bleed less freely, or a blood donor
chooses to give his blood at full moon, when he bleeds more freely.

BELOW LEFT **A page** from Albumasar's *De Magnus Conjunctionibus* shows a scholar and a knight: the scholar is supported by the glyphs of Pisces and Sagittarius, representing intellectuality and philosophy, and the knight by Scorpio and Aries, representing persistence and courage

BELOW RIGHT **An** illustration from a 13th-century edition of Bernard Silvester's *Experimentarius*, showing Euclid

At least one Arabic work played an important part in determining the philosophical attitude to astrology held by the English church: this was the *Introductorium in astronomiam* of Albumasar, translated by Herman of Dalmatia who, with Robert the Englishman (Robert of Retines), travelled in Europe in the 1140s discovering astrological works.

Albumasar's work was particularly important to those concerned about astrology's relationship to free will. He claimed that while it was certainly true that some things were unarguable – fire was hot, always had been hot, and would continue to be hot – and there was no point in contention, other elements in life were mutable: he was setting pen to paper today, but might or might not continue to write tomorrow. The planets were susceptible to reason, and their powers, divinely governed, could influence both arguable and unarguable fact.

Translations of astrological books made during the 12th century were extremely influential and widely read. Some of them became profoundly popular. Bernard Silvester, who wrote in the middle of the 12th century,

produced for instance three books, each dealing with astrology, which were very widely read indeed. Silvester's *Experimentarius* was a verse translation of a work on astrological geomancy (a means of prediction by which a number of points were dashed down at random, and then joined together by lines, creating a number of shapes then used as a key to certain constellations or sets of tables; the resident astrologer of an hotel in Agra, India, was using it still in 1982). His *Mathematicus* was a narrative poem based on an astrological prediction, and *De mundi universitate*, was about the stars themselves and their effect on the whole of creation. The latter was, in the terms of its day, a runaway bestseller, almost immediately accepted in the major schools of Europe, where interestingly there is no record of even the slightest reaction against Silvester's calling the planets 'gods' – 'gods who serve God in person' – near enough to the Creator to receive from him the secrets of the future, which they impose upon 'the lower species of the universe, by inevitable necessity'. The whole of nature derived its life from the skies, and could not move without instructions from on high – although at the same time Silvester speaks of 'what is free in the will and what is of necessity'; somewhat confusing.

The *Mathematicus* is perhaps the earliest work of fiction to depend entirely on astrology for its plot, which tells of a Roman knight and his lady whose marriage is childless. The wife consults an astrologer, who predicts that she will bear a son who will become a great genius and the ruler of Rome, but will one day kill his father. The wife tells the husband, who makes her promise to kill the child in infancy. Of course, when she becomes pregnant and gives birth to a son, she cannot bear to have him killed, and sends him away, assuring the husband that he is dead. The child, Patricida (so named to ensure that he will hate the crime of patricide) is intellectually brilliant, learning 'the orbits of the stars and how human fate is under the stars' and 'clasping divine Aristotle to his breast'. He grows up to be a brilliant soldier, too, rescuing Rome from the attacking Carthaginians, after which the king abdicates in his favour. His mother, understandably, is both pleased for her son and anxious for his father. She tells all to her husband, who to her dismay goes to Patricida and confesses how he had once ordered him to be killed, but had been overruled by the planets, which would no doubt one day order the king to kill his father. Patricida decides to commit suicide to save them both from fate; he summons the Romans together, induces them to promise him anything, and then announces that he wishes to die ... And here, alas, the intensely operatic poem breaks off, leaving us to construct our own version of what may have happened.

OPPOSITE ABOVE In the Bayeux Tapestry the recently crowned King Harold listens with foreboding as he is told of the 'Star' (Halley's Comet)

OPPOSITE BELOW On one page of a 1495 copy of the *Flores Astrologici* of Albumasar, the Sun drives his chariot proudly through the sky, while Venus is seen (RIGHT), her chariot wheels decorated with the glyph of Libra and a representation of Taurus (the signs 'ruled' by the planet). On board, the goddess of love carries blind Cupid

ISTI MIRANT STELLA

HAROLD

Ars quidem cõfiliatozes bellozṛ τ auctozes guerraṛ τ iſurgētes cõtra regē: moztē quoqz ſubitaneã cũ multitúdine iſirmitatũ: febres graues τ abſciſiones viaru̇: effuſiões ſanguini s: caſuz quoqzbuſtionis τ fluminis ʒſumptiõe Qui ſi fuerit interreſt ſignificat deſtructiõe arbozṛ per cõbuſtiõe calozṛ: τ ventos validos nocíuos τ cõbuſtiõne frugũ nouaru̇ in tempoze ſuo. Qui ſi fuerit in aere ſignificat paucitatem pluuíaru̇ τ grauitatē calozis: τ fulmína τ calozes nocíuos. Et ſi fuerit lñ ſigno aquatíco ſignificat periculoſa naufragía nauigatiũ repete cum ventís foztiter flantibus Et ſi n ſigno quadzupedũ ſignificat impedímē tum ín ínquadzupedibus quibus homínes vtunt-τ de his quepertinent ad ípm ſigno poſtea aſpice planetã inpedíente eum in quo ſigno ſit: τ com miſce locutíonē tuam ſuper hoc ſchm quod dictũ eſt in rebus h. Et ſimiliẛ eritnarratio tua ín índumento ♂ cũ malo vel foztuna ſicut ín ♄.

Sol

Ol ſignificat magnates: diuítes: τ honozabíles. Qui ſi fuerit ímpedit° hoza reuolutíonís detrimentũ patíeẛ omne q̃ eí°eſt. ita q̃ multum ímpedíenẛ: τ accídet vníuerſo vulgo: ínfir mítates. Qui ſi fuerit i̇ ſignís humanís erit ímpedímentũ ín hís q̃ ptínent ad eũ de hoíbus. Si ín terreo erit ín hís q̃ ſunt ex ſubſtantia terre τ metallo. Si fuerit ín aereo erit ímpedímentũ ín aere. Si ín aātíco q̃ ſunt ex aíalibus aquaru̇ ímpedí mentum patíeẛ nẛ. Et ſi fuerit ín loco malí foztuna verte ſentenríam τ díc loco malí bon um: τ aſpice planetam ímpedíentem eum vt ſupza.

Uenus

En°eſt ſignificatrix mulierũ ſponſalíũ. que cũ ímpedíta fuerí t hoza reuolutíoís ímpedíeẛ omne q̃ eí°eſt. Si ’n humanís ſignís ímpedímentũ patieẛ quícq̃d eíus eſt ín hoíbus. Si ín terreís q̃ ſunt ex ſubſtantia terre. Si ín aereo q̃ ſunt ín aere Et ſi ín aātíco q̃ ſunt ex ſubſtantia aā. Et ſi fuerit ín loco malí foztuna verte ſentencíã τ díc loco malí bonum: et aſpice planetã eum ímpedíentem vt ſupza.

b

609

SIGLO XV
P. BERRUGUETE
S. DOMINGO DE GUZMAN

OPPOSITE In a painting by Pedro Berruguete (d.1503), St Dominic watches as servants of the Spanish Inquisition burn books: while some are consumed, others rise in holy safety from the flames. To which category astrological works would belong we can only conjecture; the Inquisition's attitude to the subject was highly equivocal

The story was written, and taken, extremely seriously; critics who suggested that it was a satire were for the most part Christian clerics intent on producing anti-astrological polemics. There is no sign in the text itself to suggest that it was anything other than a straightforward tale, and its many readers took it as such.

England produced no astrologers to compete in reputation with some of those on the Continent, although the universities taught the subject (not with as determined a conviction as that displayed at, say, the universities of Bologna or Padua). English travelling scholars brought news of the latest developments of the study into the country – among them Alexander Neckham (1157–1215), who was a foster-brother of Richard I, born on the same night as the king, and sharing his mother's breasts with his future sovereign. He grew up to be a distinguished scholar and Abbot of Cirencester, and in his book *De naturis rerum* wrote about astrology, astronomy and natural science in general. Richard is said to have written 'something on astrology', but the manuscript has not survived.

That the peoples of Britain as a whole were affected by astrological prognostications cannot be doubted: together with most other Europeans they were thrown into a panic, for instance, by the conjunction of planets in Libra announced for 1186. Most astrologers predicted disastrous storms (Libra is an 'air' sign), with the result that many of their more credulous listeners dug underground shelters in which to pass the crisis, and services were held in many churches in an attempt to persuade the Creator to overrule the planets.

Two English writers, Roger of Hoveden and Benedict of Peterborough, attempted to comfort their hearers by recalling that an ancient astrologer, one Corumphira, had predicted that only cities in sandy regions of the earth would be affected; but Hoveden also pointed out that an English astrologer, William, clerk to John, Constable of Chester, argued that England would be included in the area of devastation as it were by divine intervention, and that 'princes should be on their guard, to serve God and flee the devil, so the Lord may avert their imminent punishments'.

As September 1186 approached, panic spread. A tract by a Saracen astrologer, Pharamella, criticizing his western colleagues' calculations, and arguing that the positions of Mars and Venus were such as to mitigate the effects of the conjunction, was too late to comfort the superstitious. As it happened, September was a rather mild and unexceptional month, and the astrologers were forced to admit that they had been mistaken: the conjunction did not provoke storms at all – instead, it instigated the victories of Saladin in the Holy Land in the following year!

As the 12th century wore on, English astrological writers continued to consolidate ancient knowledge into accepted texts. Daniel of Morley did so under the aegis of John, Bishop of Norwich; Roger of Hereford a contemporary, under that of Gilbert Foliot, Bishop of Hereford and later of London under Henry II. Daniel wrote a book dealing very thoroughly with astrology as it affected the weather, famine or plenty, events and the history of the state, with the horoscope as it revealed the life of an individual, then with its capacity for answering particular questions, and finally with 'elections', or the choosing of a moment for a particular task. The last, of course, was of use for instance when a ship's master wanted to know an auspicious moment at which to set sail on an important voyage – astrologers had already been used for centuries to predict such moments, and would continue to be used so (even by hard-headed insurers) for centuries to come.

With the 13th century came the first really notable court astrologer since Roman times of whom we have a clear record – Michael Scot, who when he died in the 1230s was astrologer to the Holy Roman Emperor, Frederick II. There is a good anecdote about Frederick II, incidentally, who during his lifetime seems to have employed a number of astrologers. When one presented himself, he decided to set him a test, and asked, 'By what gate shall I leave the castle today?' The astrologer wrote his reply, sealed it, and told the Emperor not to open it until he was outside the castle. Frederick thereupon ordered a new exit to be made in the walls, and left through the roughly cut hole. Opening the sealed message, he read: 'The king will leave today by a new way.' The astrologer was engaged.

Scot was referred to by one contemporary as 'a scrutinizer of the stars, an augur, a soothsayer, a second Apollo'. Very little is known of the life of this Scottish scholar and astrologer, but there is extensive evidence of the way in which his mind worked – a mind crammed with curious knowledge and odd theories (that, for instance, since there are fourteen joints in the fingers of the hand – and the reasons for that conclusion are not given! – man's natural lifespan should be 140 years). He discusses in a voluminous *Introduction to Astrology* the theory and practice of making use of the planets to discover God's purpose for man, addressing himself to all the old quesions – how the stars are signs, not causes, and how they can be used to discover 'something of the truth concerning every body produced in this corruptible world'. He castigates 'superstitious astrologers' (those who used numerology or geomancy), though he rather enjoys describing such occult means of divination as the shapes of clouds or the appearance of the surface of liquids.

ABOVE Michael Scot, represented in a 13th-century manuscript, was the Scottish court astrologer to the Emperor Frederick II; Dante referred to him in the *Inferno,* and he appears in Sir Walter Scott's *Lay of the Last Minstrel*

RIGHT The manuscript of one of the astrological and alchemical books by Michael Scot, which became famous all over Europe in the early decades of the 13th century

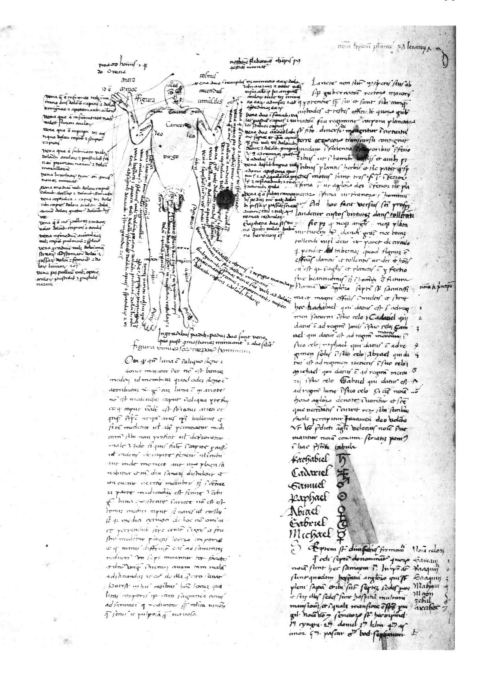

Much of Michael Scot's work is muddled and derivative, but he seems to have done some original research – on, for instance, menstruation and the phases of the Moon – and to have had a strongly felt belief that the moment of conception was, if anything, more important than the moment of birth. A woman should always, he says, note the exact time of coitus, when she may conceive, and goes into some detail about how different positions in copulation can, with the aid of the positions of the planets, have certain results at conception.

Charming magical and superstitious omens are liberally introduced into more serious astrological theories. To discover the sex of an unborn child, ask the pregnant woman to give you her hand. If she offers the right, the child will be a boy; if the left, a girl. If a man sneezes two or four times while engaged in business, and rises and walks about immediately, he will prosper in the undertaking; but sneeze twice in the night for three successive nights, and you forecast death or disaster.

Many stories of wizardry and magic grew up around the figure of Scot. A rhyme told of his peculiar powers:

> When he stampeth his foot in Spain
> The bells do ring in Notre Dame.

And people whispered of his going about by riding a demon in shape of a black horse. He is said to have foretold that he would die as the result of a blow on the head, and to avoid this always wore a steel helmet. One day, at church with the emperor, he was forced to remove it, whereupon a small stone fell on his head and killed him instantly.

Some more prominent 13th-century figures had a merely peripheral interest in astrology. But all had an interest. Albertus Magnus (1193–1280), for instance, one of the greatest scholastic philosophers of the Middle Ages, the teacher of St Thomas Aquinas, wrote little directly about astrology – yet his views on the subject come into most of his writings. Clearly, he shared the common belief that all earthly events were governed by the motions of the planets; it is asserted again and again, both obliquely and overtly. He defends free will, of course, but nevertheless asserts that a properly trained astrologer can, after studying the positions of the planets within the zodiac at the moment of birth, make predictions for the whole life of the infant – within the circumscription of what God allows. He asserts too that if an astrologer suggests a career for a boy, it will be as well to place him in it, for because of the planetary influence a special aptitude will be shown for it, as against another occupation which parents might prefer but the planets do not support. (This illustrates how astrological theory was coagulating: astrological advice about careers for children had been given before – by contemporaries of Aristotle, for instance – but was only now appearing in commentaries and textbooks.)

St Thomas Aquinas (c 1226–74), Albertus Magnus' pupil, was far less of a scientist and more of a theologian, held in high esteem by the Popes Urban IV and Clement III and canonized in 1323, less than half a century after his death, by John XXII. He took an attitude to astrology not unlike that of Albertus, denying that the stars were living beings, but claiming that no intelligent man could doubt that all natural motions of inferior bodies are caused by the movements of the planets and stars. He agreed too that many astrologers had made true predictions, if with the caveat that many others had made false ones!

Roger Bacon (1214–94), an Englishman born in Somerset and educated at Oxford, had a troublesome relationship with the Church, being twice imprisoned for heresy. He mounted a violent attack on magic and on those who pretended to practise it; but he saw that some 'magicians' were in fact scientists seriously concerned to unravel the mysteries of existence; 'scientific magic' was permissible. But he entirely accepted astrology as explained by Albertus and Aquinas, and took much their view of it, going somewhat further than them in arguing that the planets can incline men to good or bad conduct, even if both might be modified by free will.

He spent quite a lot of time considering the planets and their connection with Christianity: the connection between Mercury and Christianity, for instance – the fact that that planet is dominant in Virgo, suggesting the Virgin, and the likeness between Mercury's eccentric orbit (then so difficult to trace) and the mysterious course of the Christian creed. This theory was clearly expressed, and the Popes knew of it. Bacon was, in fact, a great believer in what we can only call astrological magic: he believed in the efficacy of verbal and real charms, for instance, if made under the proper planetary auspices, for they then stored up in them the strange energy of the stars and of the human spirit. He quotes a story of Moses escaping from a compromising amour with an Ethiopian princess by using a ring which caused her to forget him. And he claims that many of the miracles of the saints were performed by means of magic invocations spoken at the proper astrological moment.

The fact that astrology needed defending not against the Church but against some critics who put the word about that it was anti-Christian, is underlined by the publication of a work attributed to Albertus, the *Speculum astronomiae*, a lengthy defence of astrology and astronomy which seems to have been published round about 1277, at the time when Stephen, Bishop of Paris, and a number of clerical advisers published a condemnation of various opinions (219 of them, to be precise) attributed to 'Signor de Brabant, Boetius of Denmark, and others'. Many of these 'opinions' had to do with astrology – that (an old suggestion) the world would begin again when all the planets returned to their original positions at the time of the Creation; that 'the will and intellect are not moved in acts by themselves but by an eternal cause, namely, the heavenly bodies';

'that by certain signs men's intentions and changes of mind are known, and whether their intentions will be achieved; and that by such figures are known the outcome of journeys, the captivity of men, their freedom from captivity, and whether they will become sages or scoundrels'; and 'that Christianity hinders science'. Whether by intention or coincidence, the *Speculum astronomiae* answers most of them.

There are other less important and far less talented astrological writers of the period whose names survive and whose books were read for centuries, despite often considerable inaccuracies and mistakes. John Holywood of Halifax is a case in point. He was born at Halifax, studied at Oxford, and settled in Paris in about 1230; his name was latinized as Johannes de Sacro Bosco. His fame rested on a short book, *Tractatus de sphaera*, which was copied and reprinted innumerable times, and printed and reprinted in several translations from the original Latin right up until 1647 – at least forty editions within a century – even after the many astronomical errors had been pointed out. It was used by Chaucer as source material for his *Treatise on the astrolabe*, and many distinguished scholars wrote commentaries on it.

But the most important astrological book published in Latin in the 13th cemtury was the *Liber astronomicus* of Guido Bonatti, the astrologer Dante described as one of the sufferers in the fourth division of the eighth circle of the *Inferno*, among those spirits who in life had spent too much

In a 15th-century edition of Dante's *Inferno* is an illustration of a scene in which Virgil, showing Dante around the eighth circle of hell, introduces him to several men whose heads have been permanently fixed the wrong way around: a fate, he suggests, awaiting astrologers and others who attempt to foretell the future. Michael Scot was apparently among them

time trying to predict the future, and were now condemned to pace about with their heads on backwards.

Bonatti, perhaps the most famous astrologer of the 13th century, made his living by advising princes, and was for some time employed by Guido de Montefeltro. When that prince was involved in a dispute that led to military action, Bonatti would climb to the top of the campanile of his castle, and at the auspicious moment strike the bell once for the count and his men to don their armour, again for them to mount their horses, and a third time for them to ride forth to battle. Filippo Villani, a contemporary historian, claims that Montefeltro won many a battle by following his astrologer's advice.

Bonatti was absolutely forthright in his claims for his art:

All things [he said] are known to the astrologer. All that has taken place in the past, all that will happen in the future – everything is revealed to him, since he knows the effects of the heavenly motions which have been, those which are, and those which will be, and since he knows at what time they will act, and what effects they ought to produce.

His *Liber astronomicus* expresses the same modesty. He begins by stating that his book will be 'long and prolix', and indeed it is. He produced it after a lifetime's practical work as an astrologer – as a professor at the University of Bologna. His defence was opinionated, firm and pert – particularly where the opposition of some churchmen was concerned. Astrologers, he claimed, knew a great deal more about the stars than theologians knew about God, who preached about Him every day. Abraham had taught astrology to the Egyptians, Christ had used (or at least approved of using) astrology to choose propitious moments for certain tasks ('Are there not twelve hours in a day?' he had asked the disciples [John XI.9], obviously meaning that one could choose a fortunate time within them); and churchmen who said that astrology was neither an art nor a science were 'silly fools'.

Despite this, his book had some useful tips for ambitious clergymen; he lists various questions astrology can answer, and among them is whether an enquirer will ever attain the rank of bishop, abbot, cardinal – or even pope. This may of course have been a joke, although he goes on, very straight-faced, to say that while it may not be proper for a clergyman to ask such a question, many did, and an astrologer should be prepared to give an honest answer. Astrology could and should be used, too, to choose the propitious moment for starting to build a church, just as it would be when building a house or castle or city.

There remain two important European astrologers to be mentioned before the end of the century. The first, Peter of Albano, who was born in 1250, had a quiet but distinguished career. He travelled somewhat in his youth (to Sardinia and Constantinople, and allegedly to Spain, England and Scotland), spent some time at the University of Paris, where he was admired by Savanarola, then returned to Italy; was among those who met and talked to the great adventurer Marco Polo on his return from the Orient, and returned to Padua to die there in 1316, a highly paid professor.

Apart from his astrological writings, he was between 1285 and 1287 physician to Pope Honorius IV (he charged a hundred florins a day for his services, a very considerable sum), although this did not prevent him from getting into trouble with the Inquisition, which punished him after his death by disinterring him and publicly burning his bones – not because of his practice of astrology, however, but because of some unwise speculations about the raising of Lazarus (after only three days, he concluded, rather than four) and for questioning whether certain people raised from the dead by Christ and the saints might not in fact merely have been in a state of trance.

His reputation as a physician was very great, and supported by such authorities as Regiomontanus as well as by the popularity of his books on medicine. In his best-known book, the *Conciliator*, he lists over 200 questions which he has investigated, and after recalling the opinions of others, gives his own conclusions on medical matters. But elsewhere in the book he states a number of objections to astrology, and answers them with similar forthrightness, taking the standard view of the subject, underlining the fact that it is a science. Certainly, some astrologers might come to mistaken conclusions, sometimes because they were incompetent; but a good astrologer would speak the truth in most cases, and very rarely fail to be accurate in his prognostications.

As to medicine, which was his chief preoccupation, those who pursued it 'as they should, and who industriously study the writings of their predecessors, these grant that this science of astronomy is not only useful but absolutely essential to medicine.' All potions should be administered after a study of the planets' positions, and Peter goes into great detail about the theory of 'critical days' and their relation, especially, to the phases of the Moon. He discusses at some length whether blood-letting should take place at the first or some other quarter of the Moon. He certainly goes some way towards ascribing intelligence to the planets, describing one of them, on one occasion, as 'leading through all eternity a life most sufficient unto itself, nor ever growing old', and repeating a theory that associated certain angels with certain planets – Michael with the Sun, Raphael with Mercury, Gabriel with the Moon, and so on. However, he did not go far enough down the road to heresy to forgo the approval of the Pope, or during his lifetime to have any real difficulty with the Inquisition.

Cecco d'Ascoli, on the other hand, was to become famous as the only astrologer to be burned by the Inquisition. Practically nothing is known of his life and career; only that the two books which caused his execution were a poem, *l'Acerba*, and a commentary on the *Sphere* of Sacro Bosco. *L'Ascerba* is really hardly here or there – a sort of parody of Dante's *Inferno*; the *Sphere* commentary seems not in itself to be heretical. D'Ascoli affirms man's possession of free will, and offers no new or extreme astrological theories to upset the authorities. But there are one or two doubtful passages, in one of which he gives directions how the reader can make an image through which he can receive the messages of spirits (though he condemns magic).

He did from time to time refer bitingly to living people, and may well have made enemies. At all events, he was found guilty by the Inquisition at Bologna in 1324 of improper utterances, and given a fifteen day penance of confession, a daily recital of thirty paternosters and thirty Ave Marias, occasional fasting, and regular attendance at a sermon every Sunday. All his astrological books were taken from him, and he was forbidden to teach astrology, deprived permanently of his professor's chair and doctor's degree, and heavily fined.

Three years later he was again summoned before the Inquisitor – this time at Florence – found to be a relapsed heretic who had violated the terms of his sentence (how, we do not know), handed over to the secular arm, and burned with his books by Lord Jacob of Brescia. Anyone found in possession either of the poem or the commentary was automatically excommunicated.

We would probably never have heard of Cecco d'Ascoli if he had not been burned; or, perhaps, he would have survived as a mere footnote in astrological history. Ironically, he does not really seem to have perished as a result of his astrological teaching or opinions, which were in no way outrageous – nor did he make such outrageous claims as that the earth was not the centre of the universe, which would have upset the Church. Perhaps most people at the time suspected that personal enemies were responsible for his fate; it was fairly obvious that it had nothing to do with astrology. After all, his astrology was that of Aquinas and Albertus Magnus, and the first had been canonized four years before d'Ascoli's pyre was lit, while the second was shortly to be beatified.

Moreover, during the 14th century astrology was all too often

PRIMO

15

Leuante

Griego

Sirocho

Tramontana

Oftro

Maiftro

Garbin

Ponente

Li ſpiriti ſon quatro principali
Lun nien dallangiol primo allorizonte
Che in noi conſerua li atti naturali
Monſtraſe ſoa natura temperata
Fra le doe qualita actiue e zonte
Sana la terra per qual fa giornata

Li ſpiriti ſon. Q ui dicie che quatro ſono li ſpiriti cioe cierti pricipa
li.el primo uiene da oriente & queſto ſe chiama ſuſſola
no quaſi ſottol Sole uenente & queſto uento e purgato dogni malitia
da raggi del Sole perho ſignoregia alla ſtatura intra doe qualita acti
ue cioe tral caldo el freddo & intra le qualita paſſiue cioe humido &
ſeccho dale actiue cioe dal caldo al freddo ſon ſoſtenute & perho la
cita che ſottopoſta a queſto cientro e rimeſſa dalialtri:e ſana a tutti li
habitatori in eſſa & ancho e buona compreſſione & perho le camare o
uero fineſtre che ſon poſte uerſo oriente in eſſe e buona aria & buono

An illustration from an
edition of a work of
Cecco d'Ascoli, the only
astrologer burned by the
Inquisition (in 1327)

commemorated by ecclesiastical and lay authorities in permanent and respectable form to be anything but a recognizable part of the fabric of intellectual life. Look, for instance, at the capital of the eighteenth of the thirty-six great pillars supporting the lower storey of the Doge's palace in Venice, built in 1301. Ruskin described it as 'the most interesting and beautiful' capital he knew, 'on the whole, the finest in Europe'. The capitals are octagonal, and decorated by sixteen leaves; on the eighteenth capital are represented the planets in their houses, probably at the time when the cornerstone of the palace was laid.

Mars in Aries and Scorpio is particularly effective, showing a very ugly knight in chain mail with a scorpion in his hand, seated on a ram. Venus sits on a bull, with a mirror in her right hand and scales in her left (she rules Taurus and Libra); the Moon appears as a woman in a boat on the ocean, a crescent in her right hand, and drawing a crab (Cancer) out of the waves with her left. On the eighth side, God is represented creating man, his hand on the head of a naked youth.

I imagine the whole of this capital, the principal one of the old palace [Ruskin writes in *The stones of Venice*], to have been intended to signify first, the formation of the planets for the service of man upon earth; secondly, the entire subjugation of the fates and fortunes of man to the will of God, as determined from the time when the earth and stars were made, and, in fact, written in the volume of the stars themselves.

He summarized the 14th-century attitude to astrology, which was to remain constant for the next three hundred years.

VIII

'FIRST CAUSE OF MOTION, CRUEL FIRMAMENT'

THE difficulty about tracing the development of astrology is the enormous amount of evidence to be sifted. As one 20th-century writer, Don Cameron Allen, has put it, 'The literature of astrology is as vast as the history of man. No one scholar can possibly hope to untangle all of its intricately woven strands.' (*The Star-crossed Renaissance*, 1941).

Mr Allen was thinking in the main of books on the theory and practice of the subject, of 'theological' arguments; but from the 14th century onwards, there is a proliferation of comments and allusions in non-astrological literature, which has been seized upon by adherents and antagonists alike, as though to produce evidence that Dante or Shakespeare or Chaucer were 'believers' or not was to add something to the argument. Nevertheless, authors' use of astrology in their work is of enormous value, for it tells us about the general public's varied views on the subject.

It is difficult to discover, from a fictional work, the attitude towards astrology of its author; the old trap of attributing to a writer the opinions held by his characters yawns wide, and has swallowed many. And even if a writer seems to be unequivocally speaking in his own voice, there may be doubt about his motives – especially if he contradicts himself. The French poet Eustache Deschamps (*c* 1338–1415), for instance, wrote two *ballades* in which he claims that but for free will man would be completely controlled by the stars. Yet elsewhere (in his *Demonstracions contre sortilèges*) he inveighs against all sorts of divination, and makes free use of the arguments of Nicole Oresme, an opponent of astrology (of whom more later).

With Boccaccio (1313-75) as with his acquaintance, Chaucer, we come to a man whose use of astrology in his work seems as good a mirror of the general view as we are likely to find. His attitude is rather that of the serious astrologers of later generations: that is, when he says that Mars and Venus map out, in a horoscope, the sexual disposition of its subject, he is not saying that those planets actually *provoke* passion, but that through their positions at the time of birth they influence the subject's attitude to love. It would be difficult to claim Boccaccio as a proselytizer of astrology, but it certainly could not be claimed that he was a serious opponent.

Dante Alighieri (1265-1321) had clearly read the work of Boethius (see p 81), and while in the *Inferno* he condemns some astrologers, in the *Paradiso* he positively celebrated astrology as the interpreter of the will of God. Even in the *Inferno* Dante admits that the planets may make man act ('*Lo cielo i vostri movimenti inizia*'), while underlining the fact that from that moment of action he is on his own. He also believed that it was the positions of the planets that make children different from their parents, adding to inherited factors a new set of personality traits and inclinations.

Piers Plowman, for many people today the earliest accessible English poem, written by William Langland some time between 1360 and 1399, has in the earliest of its versions a sideswipe at astrology as 'evil for to know'; but the third version betrays a clear belief in the influence of the planets. It has sometimes been suggested that the slighting earlier reference was cut because of the general popularity of astrology and Langland's desire to popularize his poem. A contemporary author, John Barbour, in his 1275 poem about Robert the Bruce, mistrusts astrology on religious grounds, but on the other hand admits that the constellations can incline a man to good or evil, and that an astrologer can tell a man's character from the positions of the planets at the time of his birth.

But it is with Chaucer (c 1345-1400) that we come to the first English writer whose work is from beginning to end shot through with astrology. It is possible to argue that he made use of the subject as a selling point, as a popular ingredient in *The Canterbury Tales*; but this is not a persuasive point of view. It is much more likely that he spoke of astrological elements in the characters in his poem for the very good reason that he saw them as integral, and knew that by referring to them he made those characters more real, made their actions more credible. Which is not to say that he

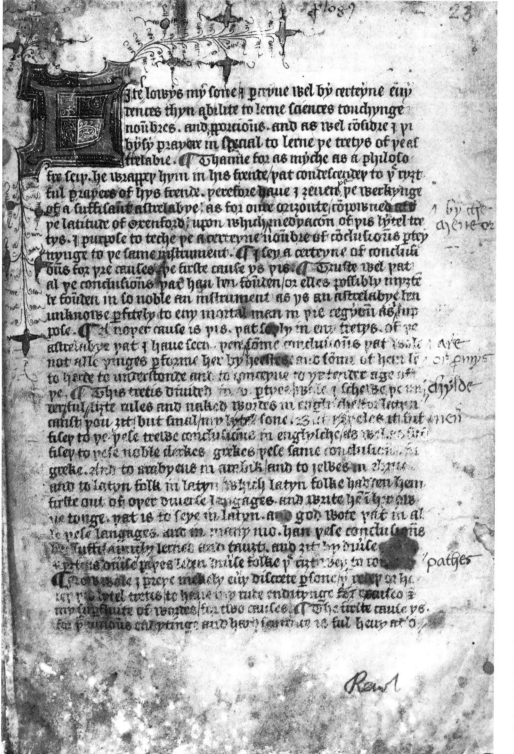

A page from Chaucer's treatise on the astrolabe. This is not so much an original work as one compiled for the use of his son Lewis from the writings of earlier authorities; it does not suggest a special sympathy to astrology as an empirical study

was an astrologer, as some have claimed, or that he was a superstitious fool, which a total acceptance of all the claims of astrology would have made him.

The Canterbury Tales (I use Nevill Coghill's modern 'translation' throughout) both opens and closes with an astrological reference: the *Prologue* announces that the pilgrimage begins when

> the young sun
> His half-course in the sign of the Ram has run . . .

and at the end of the poem, in *The Parson's Prologue*, the pilgrims approach the end of their journey as

> the power of Saturn
> Began to rise with Libra . . .

More use is made of astrology in some of the Tales than others. *The Parson's Prologue* has that one brief reference, but in *The Knight's Tale*, astrology has a crucial effect on the characters: there is a positive astrological dispute when Arcite and Palamon both ask for victory in a fight, and Arcite is promised it.

> Immediately an uproar was begun
> Over this granted boon in Heaven above
> As between Venus, fairest Queen of Love,
> And the omnipotent Mars; it did not cease
> Though Jupiter was busy making peace,
> Until their father Saturn, pale and cold,
> Who knew so many stratagems of old,
> Searched his experience and found an art
> To please the disputants on either part . . .

> 'My dearest daughter Venus,' said old Saturn,
> 'My heavenly orbit marks so wide a pattern
> It has more power than anyone can know;
> In the wan sea I drown and overthrow,
> Mine is the prisoner in the darkling pit,
> Mine are both neck and noose that strangles it,
> Mine the rebellion of the serfs astir,
> The murmurings, the privy poisoner;
> And I do vengeance, I send punishment,
> And when I am in Leo it is sent . . .

In *The Man of Law's Tale* we see an actual horoscope at work; the heroine has agreed to an arranged marriage, but the Man of Law sees that a horoscope drawn up for the moment of departure from home for her wedding reveals an unhappy future:

> First cause of motion, cruel firmament,
> Driving the stars with thy diurnal sway
> And hurling all from east to occident
> That naturally would take another way,
> Thy crowding force set heaven in such array
> That this her first, fierce journey must miscarry
> And Mars will sway this marriage, if she marry.
>
> O thou unfortunate oblique degree
> Of the Ecliptic, whence the cadent Mars,
> Thrust from his proper angle, helplessly
> Falls into Scorpio, darkest house of stars!
> O lord of war, whose influence debars
> All hope! O feeble Luna, vainly knit
> To him, thrust forth from where thou shouldest sit!
>
> And O imprudent Emperor of Rome,
> Is one time like another in such case?
> Haddest thou no astrologer at home
> To choose the favourable time and place
> For journeying? . . .

Nevill Coghill has taken certain liberties in translation, introducing the sign of Scorpio into the second verse I quote, for example. In the original this verse begins

> Infortunat ascendent tortuos,
> Of which the lord is helplees falle, alas,
> Out of his angle into the derkeste hous! . . .

This seems to mean that the Ascendant, or sign rising over the eastern horizon at the moment for which the horoscope is cast, is an unfortunate one. Since Chaucer refers to Mars, and it has a special influence when in Aries, it seems likely that that was the Ascendant. Coghill was presumably advised to bring Scorpio in because that is the sign allied to the eighth house, the house of death (traditionally also ruled by Mars). The Moon (Luna, in the Coghill version) is either in conjunction with or in aspect to Mars, the 'wicked' planet.

Versifying an astrological chart is unlikely to add to its clarity, but any astrologer reading the verses would agree that poor Custance is unlikely to enjoy a happy wedding, and indeed as it turns out she not only fails to get married at all, but just escapes massacre.

This is not the place for a detailed analysis of all the astrological allusions in *The Canterbury Tales*, but we cannot ignore the most famous, which occur in *The Wife of Bath's Tale*. Again, much play is made with the horoscope – this time the natal horoscope, drawn up for the moment of birth, rather than for some other moment of time in the life of an individual. Once again the verse abbreviates and simplifies the horoscope; not surprisingly, for a full horoscope would be far too complex to versify, or even for a poet to use in contriving a character. The Wife of Bath uses her horoscope to excuse, or at least explain, her happy sexuality:

> For Venus sent me feeling from the stars
> And my heart's boldness came to me from Mars.
> Venus gave me desire and lecherousness
> And Mars my hardihood, or so I guess,
> Born under Taurus and with Mars therein.
> Alas, alas, that ever love was sin!
> I ever followed natural inclination
> Under the power of my constellation
> And was unable to deny, in truth,
> My chamber of Venus to a likely youth.
> The mark of Mars is still upon my face
> And also in another privy place.
> For as I may be saved by God above,
> I never used discretion when in love
> But ever followed on my appetite
> Whether the lad was short, long, black or white.
> Little I cared, if he was fond of me,
> How poor he was, or what his rank might be ...

It is a vivid enough horoscope, however sketchy. The Ascendant is Taurus, and Mars is in that sign – a placing which contributes stubbornness, a hot temper, perhaps even leading to violence, sensuousness and possessiveness. Interestingly, Boccaccio (who Chaucer knew) was told by Andalò di Negro, of Genoa, that anyone born with Mars in Taurus would be 'venereal in all things', and Abholi, an Arabian astrologer, pointed out that Mars when in a 'bad' position always portended the birth of a devious person, and that Venus allied with it would produce a garrulous, mendacious virago – a reasonable description of the Wife. She herself makes the point that Venus gives her 'desire and lecherousness', though she does not say in what position the planet was; perhaps in Scorpio?

It is amusing that she refers to Mars' mark, found upon her face and elsewhere. There was often believed to be a correspondence between the horoscope and the 'marks of the body' – indeed, William Lilly, the 17th-century astrologer, believed that the truth of astrology could be usefully proved by telling someone where 'the privy marks of the body' were to be found, after merely consulting his or her birth chart; and claimed to have done it himself.

As we will find again with Shakespeare, Chaucer was able to assume that his readers had some technical knowledge of astrology – far more than any general reader today would have; they would know what was meant by allusions to the Ascendant, to planets 'in angle', to the houses, and so on.

It is certainly open to any reader to doubt whether, just because Chaucer attributes a belief in astrology to characters in a work of fiction, he necessarily accepted the theory himself. His *Treatise on the Astrolabe*, written for his son (and not, of course, a work of fiction) seems to indicate that he entirely rejected judicial astrology – the astrology that claimed to be able to foretell the future. But at the same time it suggests that he considered *astrologia naturalis* – the astrology that claims the planets affect at least some significant areas of human life – quite another matter. May it not be significant, too, that at no point in *The Canterbury Tales* does he actually condemn astrology, even judicial astrology, as stupid, or wicked, or mistaken?

It would have been difficult for Chaucer to avoid taking an interest in the subject, whatever conclusions he eventually reached about it. Few thoughtful men could escape astrology, even if they wished. Petrarch, who was certainly capable of sharp gibes about superstition, and in his letters to Boccaccio was extremely caustic about indifferent astrologers, corresponded with distinguished doctors about astrological medicine, and in a letter to the Emperor Charles IV confessed (perhaps sycophant-ically) that long ago an astrologer had promised that he would be on familiar terms with the greatest rulers of his age. Some time after his death, an historian claimed that Petrarch was himself an astrologer, and had predicted an earthquake in Tuscany and the deaths of various great men. Unlikely. But it should at least be noted that Petrarch was far harder on alchemy, magic in general, and the power of gems, than astrology.

The death at the stake of Cecco d'Ascoli signally failed to dissuade any other men from the study of astrology; and in fact it is notable that that study flourished particularly among the friars of the Middle Ages (who were not only theologians, but supporters and manipulators of the Holy Inquisition). Only a few years after d'Ascoli's execution, Niccolo di Paganica, a Dominican friar, published a book on medical astrology; he may have been the astrologer who drew up the horoscope of John the

Fearless, later Duke of Burgundy, at his birth in 1371. His book was to be found in Petrarch's library. Another Italian Dominican, Bishop Ugo de Castello, wrote and published a book on 'critical days' in 1358. This was particularly addressed to physicians, and argued that it was far more accurate to fix on the critical days of an illness by astrological means than simply to watch for physical symptoms, describing too how to fix the position of the Moon and interpret the planetary effects in the context of particular illnesses.

Some scholars made a special study of astrological medicine, and wrote voluminously on it. One such scholar was Gentile da Foligno, a severely practical man whose lectures and writings were influential. His work was not all astrological; he wrote about many aspects of medicine.

Much of Gentile's attention was given to the plague, of which he himself died in 1348. This was the notorious Black Death, and his essay on it was written at the commission of the University of Perugia just as it was attacking the city (Augustine of Trent had written on the same subject seven years earlier). It was, Gentile asserted, a sickness caused by certain planetary dispositions – most astrologers suspected eclipses of the Sun and Moon and conjunctions of Saturn and Mars as prime movers, especially when they occurred in one of the 'human' signs of the zodiac. The planets, then, it was suspected, produced a kind of rotting of the air which became poisonous when breathed into the lungs. Gentile made various suggestions for combating the plague, some based on hygiene, and extremely sensible; others based on perhaps less effective notions, such as the drinking of potable gold.

Andalò di Negro was another theorist of astrological medicine, suggesting how from the study of planetary positions you could tell whether a patient would or would not recover from an illness, what the cause of that illness was, the best times to administer laxatives, for bleeding, operating, and so on, and even suggesting, for the lay reader, the means of discovering whether the doctor attending a patient was experienced and honest, or even whether though of an evil nature he might be likely to do the patient good by accident! Interestingly enough, Andalò admits that the patient's horoscope is not likely to be helpful, because it is extremely unlikely to be accurate (the difficulty of finding out the birth time of an ordinary, undistinguished member of the general public was almost insuperable). Boccaccio thought him a splendid man, and complimented him on his grave deportment and vast knowledge of the stars, who 'since he has travelled almost the whole surface of the earth, gaining experience in every climate and under every horizon, knew by direct vision what we can only learn from gossip.'

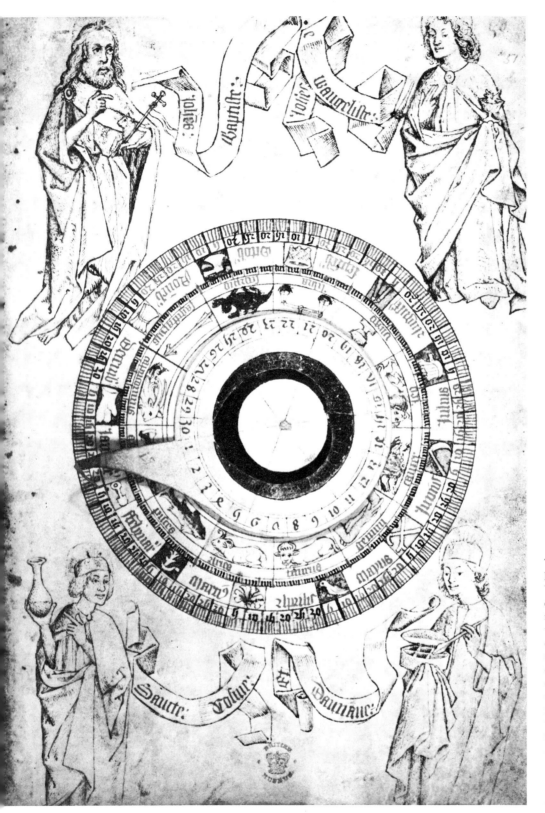

The Guild Book of the
Barber Surgeons of
York, in the 15th
century, contains a
movable vellum figure
which was of help in
computing the
astrological properties
of an illness; with
ecclesiastical blessings
from the clerics
illustrated at the top of
the page, the medical
men at its bottom were
able to prepare remedies
to be administered just
at the precise moment
when they would do
most good

Geoffrey of Meaux is said to have predicted the approach of the Black Death (although to be fair there is no actual record of this), allegedly connecting it to the appearance of a notable comet in 1315, another in 1337, and a conjunction of Jupiter and Saturn in 1325. He was obviously a man of some reputation – he is named as one of the six physicians who attended Charles IV at his coronation in 1326, magnificently clothed in fine furs at the king's expense, and taking precedence over the six surgeons who attended.

Geoffrey seems to have worked for some time at Oxford, for it is from there that he dates a work on the causes of the Black Death (in which, among other things, he suggests that because there were at the time few stars of magnitude in the sign Aquarius, the plague attacked the peasantry rather more violently than the nobility). In his work on the comet of 1337, he points out that it was generated by Mars and Saturn in Gemini, and therefore signalled infections of the blood, which suggested (since Gemini was involved) an epidemic of some kind, perhaps particularly affecting rulers and the clergy.

He gave special attention to the contagious elements of the plague, why it should attack some people and not others, why rage in one street and leave another unscathed. This was, of course, nothing to do with hygiene, but could be explained entirely by a study of the planets. As for remedy, he advised people to keep warm, not to eat or drink too much, and to encourage liberal perspiration two or three times a week. A patient could be rubbed down with a solution of linseed and camomile cooked in wine, and given spiced brandy. There is one extremely sensible piece of advice: 'Everyone should avoid standing or talking for any length of time with anybody who has the sickness, for it is contagious, poisonous and deadly in every way.'

Another strong adherent of astrological medicine was the remarkable Guy de Chauliac, born at the turn of the century, an ordinary peasant boy taken up by the local nobility and given an education. He became a canon and provost of St Just at Lyons, and physician to three Popes – Clement VI, Innocent VI and Urban V. While serving them in their palace at Avignon, he met and became a friend of Petrarch. His interest in medicine was compulsive, and among his writings is one of the most comprehensive treatises on surgery to have survived from his time. Much of his work was sound and original (he was the first surgeon we know to have used a catheter to diagnose stone in the bladder).

He, like Geoffrey, ascribed the Black Death to the 1345 conjunction of the three superior planets in Aquarius, entirely accepted the connection between various zodiacal signs and certain areas of the body, advised the use of the planets to time the administration of purgatives or bleeding, noted 'critical days', and produced such astrological aphorisms as 'A wound in the neck while the Moon is in Taurus will always be dangerous'!

Another use of astrology emphasized in the 1300s and 1400s was in weather forecasting. The meteorologists of the Middle Ages observed astronomical tables rather than barometric pressure; with agriculture playing so important a part in national economies, it was natural that astrologers should turn their attention to weather forecasting – the prediction of fine weather, storms, rain or flood. One of the earliest English astrological meteorologists was one Robert of York, a friar who lived in the first half of the 14th century (he may have died of the plague in 1345).

Robert seems to have published, at York in 1325, a work on weather prediction into which a great deal of original thought had gone; after a long preamble about the nature of the four elements and their relationship to terrestrial weather, he provides rules for predicting rain, frost, hail, snow, thunder, wind and tides, and for good measure earthquake, pestilence, wars and rebellions.

William Merlee, or Morley, a fellow of Merton College, Oxford, and a Lincolnshire rector (who died in 1347) was not only an astrological weather forecaster, but is the first Englishman of whom we hear who kept a detailed record of the weather (over seven years). Using these records, he compiled a discourse on meteorology which went into twelve chapters, in which he not only discusses the signs of good or bad weather but interprets them. It is an intensely empirical work, and Merlee makes use not only of his own observations, but those of farmers, seamen, and others depending on the weather. At least one continental European produced a parallel study: Enno of Würzburg published a very similar work during which he shows how he was able to forecast heavy snows, storms, high winds and other phenomena.

General astrological work continued at all levels: at the highest, Leo Hebreus made predictions for Pope Benedict XII and for Clement VI, and John de Murs was commissioned by the latter to produce an astrological calendar, and allegedly forecast the Pope's death in 1352. De Murs was a considerable astronomer, and agitated for calendar reform.

In England, John Eschenden (we choose, arbitrarily, one of at least fourteen alternative spellings of his name) produced a number of astrological works which are close to the almanacs that were to proliferate in the 16th century and later: he forecast such general results of astronomical activity that almost anything that happened could be verified by reference to his work. For instance, as a result of the total eclipse of the Moon of

20 March 1345, and the conjunction of the three superior planets – which according to Geoffrey of Meaux and Guy de Chauliac signalled the approach of the plague – Eschenden predicted diseases for men and beasts, death and many wars, cold, rain and snow, violent winds, rottenness in the air, worm-eaten crops, the sickness of domestic beasts, the birth of several men of genius, ill behaviour within the Church, wind and thunder, robberies, shipwrecks, drought, arson, great heat, thunderbolts and 'much cold and heat in their seasons'.

Apart from all this, serious theological argument continued, if not at very high pressure. The most notable English participant was Thomas Bradwardine (*c* 1290–1349), known as 'the profound doctor', Chancellor of Oxford University and Professor of Divinity, chaplain and confessor to Edward III, and in 1349 Archbishop of Canterbury (though he died only a month after his consecration).

In *De causa Dei*, Bradwardine advanced all the well-tried objections to astrology (more or less recapitulated from Augustine and other early authorities). But once having made it quite clear where he stood on fatalism, he put up a rather spectacular defence of astrology, totally approving Ptolemy's approach to the subject, and suggesting that it is a positive Christian duty to consider the effect the planets have on man's character, and to foster the good traits they have implanted while suppressing the evil ones. He gives the example of a merchant he once met, who confessed to him that the planets at the time of his birth indicated homosexual lust. But by application, he had overcome this. Bradwardine also quotes from a work attributed to Aristotle which told of Hippocrates visiting a physiognomist, being told that his face was that of a wanton deceiver, and admitting that he had perceived these traits in himself through a study of his horoscope, and had stifled them. Summing up, Bradwardine suggests that all theologians should study astrology, the science of celestial things and therefore the science closest to God.

This was by no means the unanimous view of all theologians. John Wycliffe (*c* 1320–84), the man who instituted the first complete English translation of the Bible, studied astrology quite closely, and apparently came to the conclusion that it was unimportant rather than positively evil. When he spoke of it, as he did in his sermons, it was as a subject which was futile; it was a waste of time for friars to study 'vain sophistry and astronomy' rather than the Bible – although it must be said that his arguments, which include an attack on astrologers for not being able to explain whether angels regulated the movements of the planets, and the accusation that Joshua's causing the Sun to stand still in the sky made a nonsense of the whole astrological theory, are not of the keenest.

A much more coherent, dangerous opponent of astrology was Nicole Oresme, a theological student from Paris who became head of the College of Navarre, and was at his death Bishop of Lisieux. He seems to have been particularly concerned at the too great reliance placed on astrology and divination by princes, though he was far from condemning the whole idea of astrology. In one short treatise he seems to be trying to prove that on the whole those princes much devoted to astrology were unfortunate in their lives; but in the same essay he carefully discriminates between 'good' and 'bad' astrology. Most opponents repeated (and still repeat) the old anti-astrological arguments. Oresme was a little more original. He argued that as it was impossible fully to predict the movements of the planets and stars, so it was obviously impossible to use them for prediction. He claimed, not producing any great body of evidence, that the Bible condemned astrology; attacked it as an inexact and often fallacious science; and claimed that, anyway, astrologers did not know nearly enough about the effects of the planets to be able to draw any firm conclusions about them.

One point he makes very clearly is one that would appeal to most modern astrologers: he disclaims any idea that the planets or stars could have any occult effect on man. If there is an influence, he says, it must be *material* – the result of light and heat, he thought. Modern astrologers would mostly say, rather, that any planetary effect is the result of some very real but so far unfathomed force (similar in nature to that of gravity), but would agree with Oresme that whatever that force is, it is certainly not occult.

He recapitulates the familiar argument about the birth of twins, the different deaths of people born at different times, and so on. As far as the mustering of a large body of argument is concerned, he seems most determined of all opponents of astrology. And yet – and this illustrates the continuing general attitude as strongly as anything – he concludes:

> I say that the prince and any other person should greatly honour true students in astrology who make tables of observations and critical rules for judgements and those who know how to consider scientifically the natures of things, discriminating the true from the false,

and consents to the propositions that many of men's actions would not take place if 'the sky' did not prompt them; that astrological weather prediction was possible (if often inaccurate), that the planets seemed to influence certain general activities such as political or religious movements. He was not an easy man to fool: when he experimented with 'elections' – the setting up of a chart for the moment of time, in order to

OPPOSITE The astrological signs take their place in a very large number of 13th-century manuscripts on all subjects

OVERLEAF LEFT Geoffrey Chaucer (c 340-1400) was among the earliest English authors to make use of astrology as a means of character delineation. The Wife of Bath, on the right, a rumbustious and lusty character in *The Canterbury Tales*, is a forthright believer in astrology, and the terms in which she describes her own horoscope show the extent of Chaucer's knowledge of the subject

OVERLEAF RIGHT With astrological medicine flourishing – it was a matter of course for centuries that no physician lacked expertise in the prescription not only of herbs and drugs, but the time at which they should be taken – most medical textbooks included an 'astrological man'. Here are four, datable 1450-1583

irgo que et iusticia appellat. ht stella
in capite obscuram ualde.1. In una
quaqz ala.1. In singlis humis siglas.
In unoqz cubito.1. In singlis manib;
siglas. In penula uestimti. 6. In una
pede.1. Sunt oms .19.

eo ht stellas in capite.3. In cuuce.
In ptore 7 in dorso 3. In sumitate
caude splendida.1. sb pectore.2. In an
tiore pede splendida.1. Sut oms .13.

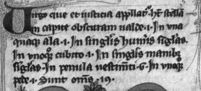

emini
p or que
dit a cante ht
stella in capite splendida.1. In utrqz hu
mo splendida.1. In utrqz genu.1. ex eoq;
Alt ht in capite stella splendida.1. In
humo siuistr.1. per singla fe
mora.1. In dorso 3. est oo.4.
In utrqz.12.

gitator ht stella in capite.1. In
utrqz humo.1. ex ea est clarioz
que in siuistr humo e.1. In utrqz cubito.1.
In dextra manu.1. In sumitate man
siuistre.2. In so ipo brachio ædulos.2. 7
In utrqz cedulo stella.1.
Sunt oms.10.

aur ht
stellas
in utrqz cornu.1.
In fronte.2. p singlos delos.1. In nare
bz e stelle pluares 7 ugille nos 7 sbbu
cile dict.1. In utrqz genu.1. In collo.2. In dor
so 3. ex qb; no
uissima splen
dida e. In ueb
.1. In pectore.1.
Sunt oms.16.

ancr ht stellas splendidas in rao. 2.
In dextris pedib;
p singlos.1. In siu
st pmo.2. 7 in siu
st tcio.1. In qrto.1.
In ore.1. In dextro
labio.2. In siuistr.2.
Sunt oms.18.

epheus ht in capite stellas splediuas
2. ex in dextr manu splendida
1. In utrqz humo.1. In zona.4. In dextr
late extuso sup illo
.4. In siuistr genu.2.
In sumitate pedu. q.
Sunt oms .21.

Quant la lune est en
cacer scorpio et pisces
il fait bō saigner au
fleumatiq. Eaue.

Quant la lune est en
taur⁹ vgo et capricor/
n⁹ il fait bon saigner
au melecoliq. Terre.

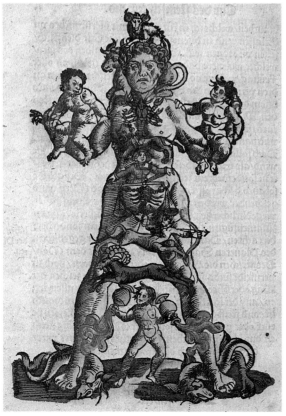

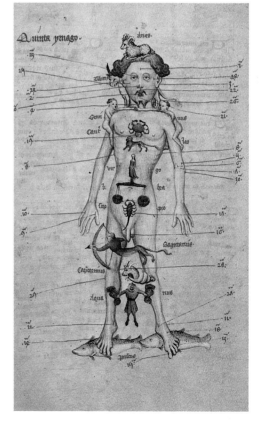

Quinta ymago.

OPPOSITE ABOVE The ravages of the plague turned many people, rich or poor, towards astrology as a means of discovering whether they or their family would survive; many astrologers claimed to be able to predict the coming of epidemics

OPPOSITE BELOW Astrological themes, particularly the signs and symbols of the planets and the gods associated with them, have always been popular as subjects for interior decorators. Pietro Perugino (1446-1523) painted in 1499 a set of beautiful frescoes in the Sala del Cambio of Perugia. Here is La Luna, with a particularly beautiful Moon goddess drawn by two handsome virgins on a chariot whose wheel, traditionally, bears the Cancer symbol (the Moon is Cancer's ruling planet)

determine an action or an attitude – and failed, he complained to an astrologer, and was told that there were factors in his own horoscope which showed that he would not be good at that aspect of the subject. 'And why', he enquired tartly and with reason, 'did you not tell me that in the first place?' The fact that despite his antagonism he was forced to conclude that there were aspects of astrology deserving respect has a certain force.

Oresme's arguments were certainly familiar to his patron Charles V of France (1337-80) – Charles the Wise, as he was called – who collected a notable library at the Louvre (it became the foundation of the Bibliothèque Royale), and whose other scholarly advisers included Raoul de Presles, Philippe de Mésières and a large number of astrologers. He was not the only monarch, of course, to find the subject of interest. When King John of France came to grief at Poitiers in 1356, he spent his subsequent captivity talking with an astrologer who had been brought by the English from Bourges because his predictions were so accurate.

The whole Hundred Years War was conducted amid a cacophony of prediction and advice from astrologers. Jacques de Saint André, a canon of Tours (later to become a friend of King John) firmly predicted the victor of Cocherel in 1364; Thomelin de Turgof, an English captain, had even earlier selected du Guesclin as the victor of Cocherel. Yves de Saint Branchier accompanied the Constable of France into battle, and selected the precise moment when he should launch his attacks. Jacques de Montciclat predicted the deaths of du Guesclin and King John. Charles the Wise himself employed Pierre de Valois of Coucy, who had also worked in England, and André de Sully, who forecast the battle of April 1366 in Spain and drew up the horoscopes of Charles' three sons, Charles, Louis and John.

But there are lesser astrologers whose names have not survived, who worked at a lower level among the troops, predicting the success or failure of this battle or of that; many of them just such cheapjacks as sprang up at the sign of any disaster, to predict illness, recovery, death, to the gullible who wanted to know what the future held.

Charles himself, whatever Oresme's attempts to wean him from reliance on the planets, seems to have conducted much of his private as well as his public life on the advice of his astrologers – who for instance drew up the horoscopes of himself and his fiancée before their marriage. He is known to have read Ptolemy, Albenragel, Guido Bonatti, as well as more modern writers, and founded a college for the study of astrology and astrological medicine at the University of Paris, giving it a good library, a fine collection of astronomical instruments, and several scholarships.

Of course there were occasional failures, some risible. On one occasion astrologers ordered a knight to prepare his arms for a duel at a particular moment of time which would ensure his success. He did so, only to find that at the moment when the conflict was to begin, it poured with rain, and the whole thing was called off. Well, at least he escaped death or injury, which was success of a sort.

As the 14th century ends, there is still no real sign of a diminution of the powers of astrologers. The French and English courts, the Bohemian court, the German court all relied on them to some extent, and it is difficult not to see serious attacks on them as uncharacteristic and even eccentric – except for jokes at the expense of the over-credulous; such as that of Sebastian Brant, in his *Das Narrenschiff* (*Ship of fools*), first published in 1494 in Basel. This long satirical work sees the whole world as populated by fools, and attacks dishonest cooks, crooked lawyers, jerry-builders, blasphemers, cheating tradesmen, adulterous wives, with equally splenetic vigour. Astrologers, or 'star-gazers', were among his targets (as these lines, from William Gillis's translation, illustrate):

> The stars, they say, aren't independent,
> Events both great and small attendant
> Upon them; every flea-brain notion
> Is read in each celestial motion:
> What he should say and what advise.
> And will his fortunes sink or rise,
> His plans, his actions, well or sick –
> Outrageous hocus-pocus trick.
> The world, which grows more stultified,
> To trust in fools is satisfied.
> The traffic in these divinations
> Appeals to printers' inclinations;
> They print as much as fools can bring,
> Each shameful word dolts say or sing.
> The public's failure to reprove it
> Must witness that the folk approve it ...

IX

SUCCESS - AND THE BEGINNING OF FAILURE

D URING February 1524 there was a conjunction of all the planets in the water sign of Pisces. One Johann Stoeffler of Justingen noted in his 1522 almanac that this was nothing to look forward to, for 'in the month of February will occur twenty conjunctions, small, mean and great, of which sixteen will occupy a watery sign, signifying to well-nigh the whole world, climates, kingdoms, provinces, estates, signitories, brutes, beasts of the sea, and to all dwellers on earth indubitable mutation, variation and alteration such as we have scarce perceived for many centuries from historigraphers and our elders.'

If Stoeffler was the first astrologer to warn of this coming planetary activity, others were not slow to follow; over fifty of them published more than a hundred books and pamphlets worrying the fact over, many prophesying the second Flood, although some took a more moderate view. Agostino Nifo, for instance, suggested that while there was certainly likely to be more rain than usual, Jupiter's predominance over Saturn strongly suggested that this would be beneficial rather than destructive; there certainly might be flooding, however, and a watch should be kept. On the whole, the more serious-minded astrologers agreed with him, leaving prophesies of deluge and disaster (often linked with war and bloodshed) to sensation mongers, of whom there were plenty.

February 1524 passed in fair weather. The astrologers of Bologna, where the university supported a strong astrological faculty, were distinctly surprised. However, their mistake seemed to be one of timing, or

perhaps it was simply that the effects of the conjunction were slow to be felt, for on 19 March there was heavy rain in the city, and from 12 May prayers were said continuously for three days in an attempt to stop the torrent. On 21 May, the citizens rang the bells in the steeples of Bologna in an attempt to mitigate the effects of the storms; four days later they were rung twice in one day, and on 12 June rung again. That night there was an hour-long storm of such ferocity that the citizens were terrified. On 30 June the bells once more fought the wind, and on 14 July the clergy struggled through a thunderstorm to ring them again. On 20, 22 and 23 July, they were rung in an attempt to break up a storm during which hailstones as big as hens' eggs pelted the streets.

At the end of August houses had to be abandoned because of the floods, which drowned much farm stock. There were prayers against rain in September, during October and November streams and rivers overflowed and dowsed the countryside, and it was not until December that the rains finally subsided. Far from announcing that they had told the people so, the astrologers began to quarrel among themselves as to why they had not been able to predict more accurately the course of the storms.

During the 16th century astrology more than ever commanded the attention of the Popes. Just after the turn of the century, Julius II was receiving predictions from Antonio Campanazzo. Leo X (1513-21, the son of Lorenzo de' Medici, the Magnificent) relied greatly on his personal astrologer, Franciscus Priulus, who wrote a whole book about his patron's birth chart, and had apparently been able to tell the Pope many facts about his childhood which only he had known. Leo always claimed that Priulus was able to make predictions accurate to the very day; and all in all it must have been a considerable shock when the astrologer killed himself – an act in the commission of which he showed great determination, for failing to drown himself, jump into a fire, cut his throat with a scythe and jump out of a window, he finally starved himself to death. Leo then turned for advice to Pellegrino Prisciano of Ferrara, Thomas Philologus, Castaneolus, Nifo and Bernard Portinarius.

Leo's successors, Adrian VI and Clement VII, at the least allowed astrological almanacs to be dedicated to them. Paul III (1534-49) positively encouraged astrologers to come to Rome and work under his protection, and on assuming the pontificate installed as unofficial astrologer to the papacy the well-known practitioner Luca Gaurico, who he made a bishop. Gaurico engaged in various minor controversies about the life of Jesus (the date of the crucifixion, the number of hours between it and the resurrection, and so on), but was used by the Pope in the main for such practical matters as electing the precise time at which the

OPPOSITE **The astrologer Paris Ceresarius of Mantua foretold the election of Paul III to the papacy. The Pope (here painted by Titian) knighted another astrologer, Luca Gaurico, with whom he regularly dined, and then made him Bishop of Giffoni. His physician, Andrea Turino, dedicated to him a book on astrological medicine**

cornerstone of new buildings in the neighbourhood of St Peter's should
be laid (the astrologer turned up in great pomp, with a splendidly robed
assistant, Vincentius Campanatius of Bologna, to cry out in a loud voice
when the moment had arrived, when a cardinal laid the marble slab).

It must be admitted that Pope Paul III's personality was not such that
his devotion to astrology can be claimed as contributing to its respectability, for he claimed the efficiency in amorous affairs of a unicorn's
horn purchased for 12,000 gold pieces, was extremely superstitious, and
addicted to chiromancy. He also had the ill grace to die twelve years
earlier than the year elected for that event by his last astrologer, Marius
Alterius. Alterius' prediction that he would live to be a hearty 93 was no
doubt part of a general scheme to keep the old man happy – how else to
explain the prediction that a Pope in his 83rd year would experience
in 1548 a year of success with women, who would bring him erotic
diversions 'which will overwhelm your spirit with singular pleasure'?

Paul's favourite, Gaurico, had a notable school of astrology at Ferrara,
where he tutored many of the century's best-known astrologers. Astrology was taught not only at private schools but at the universities; perhaps
the best example of this in the 16th century was to be seen at Bologna,
whence the professors sent forth many annual volumes of predictions.
Between 1501 and 1528 Jacobus Benatius lectured on astrology daily,
together with a colleague, Iacobus Petramellarius, a doctor in arts and
medicine who had taught astrology there since 1496.

No one at Bologna would have thought of wasting time arguing for
the intellectual respectability of astrology. This was now taken for
granted, and at most there was an occasional sarcastic thrust at 'those
who persuade themselves that a most noble body such as the sky effects
nothing in these inferiors but produced merely light, and through light,
heat.' Elsewhere there was a similar attitude. At the University of Paris
astrology was so thoroughly embedded in the curriculum that in 1512
Gaurico was seriously thinking of leaving Italy and going to Paris to
work, on the grounds that the university there was more thoroughly
committed to it. Indeed there was a lengthy tradition, and in 1437 the
university had decreed that all physicians and surgeons must possess a
copy of the current almanac for use as a medical textbook. Jean Avis
produced annual almanacs for the medical faculty for forty years. Yet
historians have claimed that the theological faculty at Paris was
opposed to the teaching of astrology, which was never the case.

Many monarchs of Europe competed for the services of Regiomontanus (1436–76), an immensely distinguished astronomer and astrologer,
and in France Nostradamus (1503–66), whose fame rested and still rests

OPPOSITE
Nostradamus, or Michel
de Notre-Dame (1503-
66) was a Jewish French
astrologer for whose
skill in combating the
great plagues of Lyons
he can be forgiven much.
Though he was well
known for his
astrological prowess,
there are no real means
of knowing how expert
he was in the field; he is
much better known as a
clairvoyant whose
prophesies seem to have
been simple hunches,
and are couched in
symbolic form

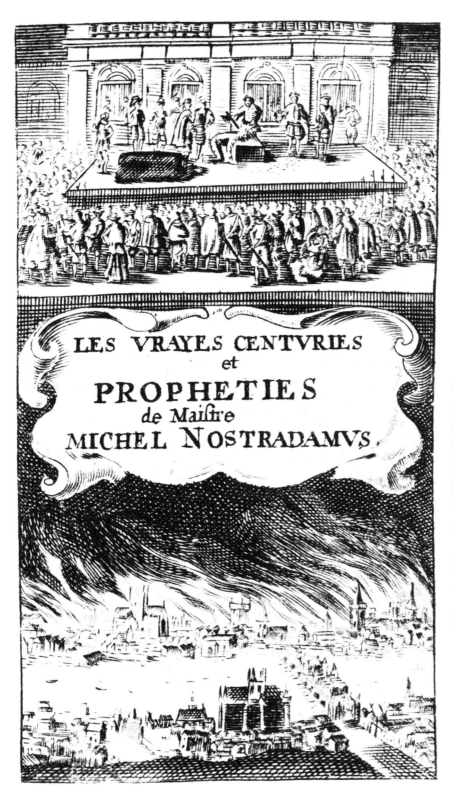

LES VRAYES CENTVRIES
et
PROPHETIES
de Maiſtre
MICHEL NOSTRADAMVS

A page from the *Centuries* of Nostradamus, a series of rhymed verses so vaguely phrased that they could be, and often are, twisted into prophesying anything. During the Second World War, Heinrich Himmler employed an astrologer to translate those quatrains which seemed to foretell the defeat of Britain. In an earlier age, during the 17th century, a French edition of the *Centuries* was alleged to have foretold the execution of Charles I and the Great Fire of London

OPPOSITE Pope Leo X (painted here by Raphael) consulted in 1520 the astrologer Dominicus Maria Castaneolus, who told him that he would triumph over all enemies, gather much gold, and prudently increase his domain. He made much money by selling cardinal's hats and membership of the Knights of St Peter, made the Holy See supreme in all Italy, and restored papal power in France

CATHERINE DE MÉDICIS
CHEZ SON ASTROLOGUE

Le Jeudi 7 Novembre (1577), commença
à paroistre une comette vers le midy. Ces
fols d'astrologues disoient qu'elle présageoit la
mort d'une royne. Ce que ayant entendu la royne
mère entra en frayeur et appréhension que ce
fust elle...

L'ESTOILE

E. BLANCHE.

OPPOSITE **Catherine de'Medici (1519-89)** is said to have embraced astrology during her years of obscure poverty, before her marriage to Henry II of France. In 1914, Jacques Emile Blanche illustrated a visit to her astrologer, Ruggieri, for a French almanac

BELOW LEFT The astrologer Lariviere was summoned by Henry IV of France to attend the birth of the baby who became Louis XIII

BELOW RIGHT **Jean Baptiste Morin**, physician and Royal Professor of Mathematics at Paris

on gnomic pronouncements of future doom couched in symbols so obscure that any interpretation can be placed on them, led a group of astrologers which much influenced Henry II's widow, Catherine de' Medici. Henry IV ensured that an astrologer was present at the birth of his son, the future Louis XIII, who in turn ordered Jean Baptiste Morin (1583-1656) to attend at the birth of his son, the future Louis XIV. Later, Morin hid behind the curtains of the royal bedroom to observe the precise moment at which the young Louis XIV and his bride consummated their marriage, so that he could work out the conception horoscope of any future Dauphin who might be born as a result of the coupling.

In Spain, an astrologer advised Philip II against a planned visit to Mary Tudor in England, on the grounds that his charts showed a deep plot against Philip. (In England, as we shall see, Mary had her own astrological adviser.) Rudolf II, the Hapsburg Emperor, was patron of several astrologers. And in England, the tradition started by the Conqueror continued, for most monarchs had an interest in the planets and their auguries. Henry VI consulted a Master Welch about the time of his coronation, and later engaged Richard de Vinderose, an Englishman trained in France, as his court astrologer. Edward IV favoured a Master Eustache,

HIERONYMI CAR
DANI, PRÆSTANTISSIMI MATHE.
MATICI, PHILOSOPHI, AC MEDICI,
ARTIS MAGNÆ,
SIVE DE REGVLIS ALGEBRAICIS,
Lib.unus. Qui & totius operis de Arithmetica, quod
OPVS PERFECTVM
inſcripſit, eſt in ordine Decimus.

HAbes in hoc libro, ſtudioſe Lector, Regulas Algebraicas (Itali, de la Coſ
ſa uocant) nouis adinuentionibus, ac demonſtrationibus ab Authore ita
locupletatas, ut pro pauculis antea uulgò tritis, iam ſeptuaginta euaſerint. Ne=
q́ ſolum, ubi unus numerus alteri, aut duo uni, uerum etiam, ubi duo duobus,
aut tres uni æquales fuerint, nodum explicant. Hunc aũt librum ideo ſeor=
ſim edere placuit, ut hoc abſtruſiſſimo, & planè inexhauſto totius Arithmeti
cæ theſauro in lucem eruto, & quaſi in theatro quodam omnibus ad ſpectan
dum expoſito, Lectores incitarētur, ut reliquos Operis Perfecti libros, qui per
Tomos edentur, tanto auidius amplectantur, ac minore faſtidio perdiſcant.

Girolamo Cardan, the Italian physician, mathematician and astrologer, was the illegitimate son of a well-known Milan jurist. He became Professor of Mathematics in that city. The author of an excellent treatise on algebra, he was best known for his work on astrology; towards the end of his life he was imprisoned for attempting to cast the horoscope of Christ and Henry VII and Edward VI relied on two Italians, William Parron and the famous Jerome Cardan (1501–76), mathematician and physician as well as astrologer, the first man to suggest teaching the blind to read by touch, who for some time attended Archbishop John Hamilton at St Andrews. In the 1520s, John Robyns, a Fellow of All Souls, Oxford (and later chaplain to Henry VIII and canon of Christchurch and Windsor) addressed his king on the matter of comets, and even went to Woodstock and Buckingham to continue discussion of the matter with Henry, himself no mean mathematician, and so able to follow the astronomical calculations. The king was far from unsympathetic to astrology, positively precluding his bishops from preaching against it, and accepting advice from a visiting German astrologer, Nicholas Kratzer, as well as from Robyns. Whether or not Cardinal Wolsey actually set up Henry's chart in order the better to curry favour with him is not proven, but rumour certainly had it so, and Wolsey took astrological advice in other matters.

After Henry's death, Cardan came to England expressly to calculate the chart of Edward VI (and incidentally that of his tutor John Cheke); the Secretary of State, Sir William Paget, received the dedication of a book by Bonatus, and Sir Thomas Smith, who was to become Secretary

The horoscope of Henry VI of England, published by Cardan in 1578, twenty-five years after the king's death

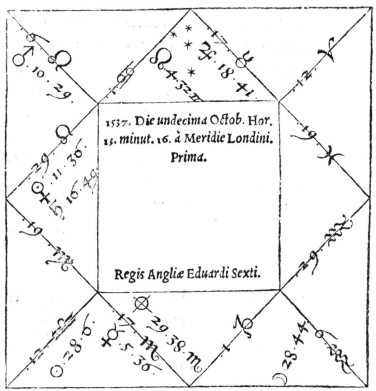

1537. Die undecima Octob. Hor. 15. minut. 16. à Meridie Londini. Prima.

Regis Angliæ Eduardi Sexti.

of State, was so taken by astrology that he could 'scarce sleep at night from thinking of it'.

There was little opposition: astrology was still occasionally a matter for satire or blunt humour, but the greatest minds of the time were at least open on the subject. Sir Thomas More made a few weak jokes (about the astrologer who could not predict his wife's infidelity, for instance, and such childishness) but went no further. Erasmus, on the other hand, always eager to attack superstition, not only consulted astrologers but even himself invoked the planets (as, for instance, the cause of certain intellectual disputes at the University of Louvain in 1519).

And what of the great astronomers? – for we are, after all, in the century of Copernicus, Tycho Brahe, Kepler and Galileo. They regarded astrology as part of their discipline; they could set up and interpret astrological charts, and to some extent used astrology either to gain knowledge (as they saw it) or to make money.

The Polish astronomer Nicolaus Copernicus (1473–1543), whose *De revolutionibus orbium coelestium* put forward in 1543 the theory (far from a new one, of course) that the Sun was at the centre of the planetary system, had astrological works in his library, and well-thumbed ones at that. *De revolutionibus* is entirely astronomical, with not a word of astrology in it, and critics have made much of this; but after all, there is not a word of astrology in Ptolemy's *Almagest*, which did not inhibit him as author of the *Tetrabiblos*.

The appearance of a bright new star in the skies in November 1572 provoked Tycho Brahe (1546–1601) to spend a great deal of time in astronomical and astrological speculation. He wrote several pages on its astrological significance, which he thought would be greater than that of any previously experienced conjunction of planets. He thought it probably signalled considerable political upheaval, and perhaps religious changes. His considerable interest in astrology seems to have been sharpened by the new star. Lecturing on mathematics to the University of Copenhagen two years later, he spent much of his time defending astrology, and arguing that while it was not a science which could be compared for certainty of effect with those of geometry or astronomy, it was none the less one it would be foolish to discount. As the years went on, his interest continued, and even increased. He drew up birth charts for members of the Danish royal family, making his own astronomical observations on which to base them, rather than relying on existing ephemerides. He had some doubts about the dubious practice of assigning zodiacal influences to cities or countries, but apparently none about the human significance of the planets' positions at birth.

DIALOGO
di
GALILEO GALILEI LINCEO
AL SER.^{mo} FERD. II. GRAN. DVCA. DI
TOSC ANA

Stefan. Della Bella. F.

The frontispiece of a work dedicated by Galileo to his patron Ferdinand de'Medici, the ruling Grand Duke of Tuscany, through whose offices he was in 1592 appointed to the Chair of Mathematics at the famous University of Padua. The engraving shows Galileo, on the left, in discussion with Ptolemy and Copernicus

The German astronomer Johannes Kepler (1571-1630) was always fascinated by astrology: his own 'horoscope book', which he kept religiously as a student, has given us most of our information about his early years. At Graz, in 1594, he took up the post of teacher of mathematics and astronomy, and there produced four annual almanacs - for which he was paid 20 florins a time, a useful addition to an annual salary of only 150 florins. He was either a very good astrologer or a very fortunate man, for in his first almanac he phophesied very cold weather and an invasion by the Turks. Both duly occurred: it was so cold (he assured a correspondent) that people died of it; when they blew their noses, those noses fell off. At the same time, promptly on 1 January, the Turks marched in, destroying much of the country between Vienna and Neustadt.

For the rest of his life, whether he liked it or not (and though he occasionally protested, there is no real evidence that he was seriously concerned) he was to some extent a professional astrologer. Some of his apparently anti-astrological gibes are well-known: the one about astrology being the stepdaughter of astronomy, or about his being forced by economic necessity to put a foot into a dirty puddle. But these seem born of impatience rather than anything else, and there is no doubt that he took the subject seriously. In the introduction to *Tertius interveniens* he warns readers that while justly rejecting the stargazers' superstitions, they should not throw out the baby with the bathwater, for

nothing exists nor happens in the visible sky that is not sensed in some hidden manner by the faculties of Earth and Nature, [so that] these faculties of the spirit here on earth are as much affected as the sky itself.

Kepler puzzled over the nature of the planetary effect on man for the rest of his life, never ceasing to inveigh against the quacks, but never for a moment doubting that within what he saw as a very debased science, a grain of truth resided – and more than a grain: his attitude in general was that the planets gave a general shape to man's character,

in the manner of loops which a peasant ties at random around pumpkins in a field; they do not cause the pumpkin to grow, but they determine its shape. The same applies to the sky: it does not endow a man with his habits, history, happiness, children, riches or a wife, but it moulds his condition ...

In England, the only man whose mind could be compared with that of Kepler or Brahe was that astonishing Elizabethan John Dee (1527–1608). Had he resisted a fascination with magic, his reputation would stand higher than it does; even so, no one doubts his accomplishments as a navigator, a mathematician and a philosopher, even if in the end his adventures into the occult led him into the hands of the master-quack Edward Kelley, and the barren fields of alchemy and angel-raising.

Dee was born at Mortlake, the son of a minor servant at the court of Henry VIII. He showed an early mathematical bent, and after a primary education at school in Chelmsford went up to St John's, Cambridge, and

John Dee (BOTTOM RIGHT) the great Elizabethan magus − geographer, magician, astrologer. It was the influence of Edward Kelley (TOP LEFT), chiefly interested in alchemy and magic, that was largely responsible for his intellectual decline during the second half of his life. Dee was much influenced by the work of Roger Bacon (TOP RIGHT), the English philosopher and scientist said to be interested in 'the black arts', and by that of Paracelsus (BOTTOM LEFT), the highly individual physician whose enquiry into alchemy specially fascinated Dee

there studied intensively − and also laid the foundations of his reputation as a magician by devising a flying machine for a college production of Aristophanes' *Pax* so real that the audience suspected witchcraft.

His major interests were mathematics and navigation, and he went on to study them at the University of Louvain. The study of navigation obviously required dexterity in mathematics, and in astronomy, and Dee claims that by the time he left Cambridge for Louvain he had already 'taken thousands of observations of the heavenly influences and operations in this elemental portion of the world'. But at Louvain his reputation was as a logician; many distinguished men were soon travelling to the university to hear him lecture. Back in England − via Paris and Rheims, where he also lectured with enormous success, students perching half-way up the walls of the college to hear him − he accepted a pension of a hundred crowns a year from Edward VI, and achieved the patronage of the Duchess of Northumberland, whose husband was Chancellor of Cambridge University.

It was at this time, in the 1550s, that we first hear of Dee as a caster of horoscopes; he may have begun to use them as part of a general interest in medicine. At all events, his diaries begin to be full of charts and notes upon them, some amusing:

Mrs Brigit Cook, born about seven of the clock on St David's Day, which is the first day of March, being Wednesday, but I cannot yet learn whether it was before noon or after. But she thinketh herself to be but 27 years old . . . but it cannot be so.

Dee's view of astrology was very much that of Kepler: it was

an art mathematical, which reasonably demonstrateth the operations and effects of the natural beams of light, and secret influences of the stars and planets, in every element and elemental body at all times in any horizon assigned . . .

Man's body, and indeed all terrestrial bodies, he believed, were

altered, disposed, ordered, pleasured and displeasured by the influential working of the Sun, Moon and other stars and planets.

His interest in the subject was to be almost as much the cause of history's neglect of him as a scholar, as his interest in alchemy and the occult in general. It was also to lead him into considerable trouble at the beginning of his career. True, Mary Tudor showed some sympathetic interest in him, and announcing that she would be his patron, invited him to draw up her horoscope and that of her prospective husband, Philip of Spain, and compare the two (a work of *synastry*, as astrologers call chart comparison of this sort).

But Dee was not drawn to Mary, whether because his charts warned him off, or because of the execution of Northumberland, the husband of his patroness, and her persecution of the Protestants. For whatever reason, he was soon exchanging secret messages with her sister, Princess Elizabeth, then in virtual captivity at Woodstock. Dee was a cousin of Elizabeth's nurse, Blanch Parry, still her maid and with Parry's help he sent and received messages from Woodstock.

The dangers inherent in the situation hardly need emphasis, and Dee went on to an even more dangerous course: that of sending Elizabeth the horoscope of the Queen, and pointing out contrasting elements in the two charts. Roman astrologers had been executed for less, and when rumours of Dee's tactlessness got out, it is not surprising that informers accused him of involvement in a plot to murder the Queen. In the spring of 1555, various members of the Princess's household were arrested and accused of witchcraft, 'for that they did calculate the King's, the Queen's and my Lady Elizabeth's horoscopes'. Dee was taken, his rooms searched, his papers read; he was charged with treason and worse – that he had a familiar spirit which had attacked both of the children of one of his accusers, Ferrys, striking one blind and the other dead.

Even in those superstitious times, the second charge seems to have been thought a little much, for the Star Chamber acquitted Dee, releasing him into the custody of Bishop Bonner of London, who was commanded to examine him on his faith. He spent some time sharing a small cell with a heretic, Barthlet Green, who was taken out and burned at the stake. Bonner seems to have been unable to shake Dee, however, for he was eventually released. Unsurprisingly, he failed to find favour again with the Queen. Incautiously, he even renewed contact with Elizabeth, and seems to have encouraged her, during Mary's last illness, to expect the succession. When Mary died in 1558 and Elizabeth indeed became Queen, one of her first acts was to commission Lord Robert Dudley, later the Earl of Leicester, to go privately to Dee and ask him to propose an auspicious date for her coronation. She accepted his proposal of Sunday, 15 January without question; and if the chart for that day promised well for her reign, it did not lie.

There has been much speculation as to the amount of work Dee did for Elizabeth, not only as astrologer but (as some biographers have proposed) as secret agent; amusingly, he signed his reports to her with a symbol that was meant to represent a pair of eyes, but looks suspiciously like *007*. There is no doubt of the value of his work as a navigator, advising Elizabethan adventurers and explorers. And there is plenty of evidence that he taught astrology, among other things (chemistry, for instance). Among his pupils was Sir Philip Sidney, whose attitude to the subject comes out in one of his sonnets:

> Though dusty wits dare scorn astrology,
> And fools can think those lamps of purest light
> Whose numbers, ways, greatness, eternity,
> Promising wonders, wonder do invite
>   To have for no cause birthright in the sky
> But for to spangle the black weeds of night;
> Or for some brawl, which in that chamber hie,
> They should still dance to please a gazer's sight;
>   For me, I do Nature unidle know,
> And know great causes, great effects procure:
> And know those bodies high reign on the low ...

Dee's analysis of Sidney's character through his horoscope (drawn up when Sidney was 16 or so) is interesting, underlining great promise in rhetoric, dialectic, natural philosophy, grammar and ethics, and describing him as a promising young man 'intended by nature for the study of the mathematicals, and by birth for learning celestial philosophy'.

Several things about Dee's life-style and career seem to support the theory that he was more than an astrologer to Elizabeth – that he provided her with political information gleaned during his European travels. She did consult him about various astronomical phenomena which appeared during her reign, and occasionally dropped in at his house at Mortlake to look at some new book (he had the finest library in the country, and one of the best in Europe) or to examine some new toy: there is a strange description in his diary of her visiting him within four hours of his first wife's death, and of the company being convulsed with laughter at the effects of his new 'magic glass' – probably a concave mirror. But she also must have given him considerable sums of money, for he lived in great state – the Mortlake house was a large one, he bought many expensive books, and built no less than three laboratories for his chemical and alchemical experiments. The poverty that always dogged him was due to his living determinedly above his means, rather than to lack of funds.

Even the Queen's protection failed to prevent Dee's being attacked; the odour of witchcraft clung to him. Not long after Elizabeth's accession, Bishop Jewell publicly sermonized against him, and John Foxe, in his 1563 *Acts and Monuments*, referred to him as 'Dr Dee the great Conjurer', a 'caller of devils'. Foxe was forced to strike the libellous reference out of later editions, but the damage was done; and Dee was to make matters worse by devoting much of the rest of his life to alchemy and conversations with angels, held in the company of his new associate Kelley, a disreputable scoundrel who among other things relayed to the reluctant Dee instructions from one angel that their wives should be held in common – a proposal that failed to appeal to Mrs Dee.

Dee's interest in astrology lasted his lifetime – in 1603 and 1604 he was casting the horoscopes of his grandchildren, and predicting for his eldest son great fortune won at the hands of a foreign prince (which turned out to be entirely true, for the boy was to become the personal physician of Tsar Mikhail Fyodorovich Romanov). But sadly, the unfavourable reputation he acquired during the last twenty years of his life outweighed the value of his work for the state, to say nothing of his serious interest in astrology; and finally, he probably contributed to the atmosphere which was to encourage the approaching desuetude of astrology.

It is frequently suggested that Dee was the original of Shakespeare's

OPPOSITE **Queen Elizabeth I was specially fond of John Dee, who calculated the most propitious time for her Coronation, and (he wrote) 'promised unto me great security against any of her kingdom that would by reason of any my rare studies and philosophical exercises unduly seek my overthrow'**

Prospero, which may or may not have been the case; it is reasonable to assume that Shakespeare would have encountered Dee in the small world of 16th-century London, and he may have given him some information about Bermuda, the isle of *The Tempest*. Shakespeare was as interested in astrology as any other Elizabethan; indeed anyone who wants to know just how the average citizen felt about the subject can do far worse than go to the plays.

During the reign of Elizabeth astrology became more firmly a part of the intellectual structure of England than at any other time in its history. Scarcely any intelligent man spoke out against it except in its most superstitious aspects, and most regarded it as a manifestation of the means by which God regulated earthly matters. The naturalness and

Like almost every educated man of his age, Sir Walter Raleigh accepted astrology as part of the scheme of structure of the solar system, and expressed this belief tellingly in his great *History of the World*, written during his imprisonment in the Tower of London and published in 1614, four years before his shameful execution pervasiveness of this belief comes out in many areas of the literature of the time – succinctly in Walter Raleigh's *History of the World*:

And if we cannot deny but that God hath given virtue to spring and fountain, to cold earth, to plants and stones, minerals, and to the excremental parts of the basest living creatures, why should we rob the beautiful stars of their working powers? For, seeing they are many in number and of eminent beauty and magnitude, we may not think that in the treasury of His wisdom which is infinite, there can be wanting, even for every star, a peculiar value, virtue and operation; as every herb plant and flower adorning the face of the earth hath the like. For as these were not created to beautify the earth alone and to cover and shadow her dusty face but otherwise for the use of man and beast to feed them and cure them; so were not those unaccountable glorious bodies set in the firmament to no other end than to adorn it but for instruments and organs of His divine providence, so far as it hath pleased His just will to determine?

That Shakespeare shared this view is a reasonable assumption, even remembering the danger of assuming that he put his own views into the mouths of his characters. It is difficult for instance not to believe that we are hearing his voice through that of Ulysses in the great speech on degree in *Troilus and Cressida*:

> The heavens themselves, the planets, and this centre,
> Observe degree, priority, and place,
> Insisture, course, proportion, season, form,
> Office, and custom, in all line of order:
> And therefore is the glorious planet Sol
> In noble eminence enthron'd and spher'd
> Amidst the other; whose med'cinable eye
> Corrects the ill aspects of planets evil,
> And posts, like the commandment of a king,
> Sans check, to good and bad: but when the planets
> In evil mixture, to disorder wander,
> What plagues and what portents! what mutiny!
> What raging of the sea! shaking of earth!
> Commotion in the winds! frights, changes, horrors,
> Divert and crack, rend and deracinate
> The unity and married calm of states
> Quite from their fixture!

Shakespeare's audience would have followed that speech with an instant grasp even of the technicalities. Most members of a modern audience need a footnote to explain what 'ill aspects' are, for instance; Shakespeare knew that his audience would understand, just as they would understand the other technical references in the plays, which often convey jokes missed by 20th-century audiences. Elizabethan playgoers also instantly understood what the playwright was doing when he put all the attacks on astrology made in the plays (not that there are many of these) into the mouths of fools like Launcelot Gobbo or villains like Edmund, in *Lear*. Modern critics quote Edmund's speech near the beginning of the play as Shakespeare's denigration of astrology, mocking 'the excellent foppery of the world, that when we are sick in fortune, often the surfeit of our own behaviour, we make guilty of our disasters the Sun, Moon and stars', and going on to claim that he, Edmund, 'should have been that I am, had the maidenliest star in the firmament twinkled on my bastardising.' What they miss, but the Elizabethans would have grasped, is that Shakespeare uses this very speech as a shorthand signal of Edmund's villainy.

Not that Shakespeare is not happy to make fun of the astrological quack (as when Antipholus of Ephesus describes Dr Pinch, in *The Comedy of Errors*, as 'a mere anatomy, a mountebank/A threadbare juggler, and a fortune-teller') and in another passage, often misunderstood – Cassius' famous lines from *Julius Caesar*, in which he tells Brutus that

> Men at some time are masters of their fates.
> The fault, dear Brutus, is not in our stars,
> But in ourselves, that we are underlings.

That is, men must take the right moment (which any competent astrologer would propose) at which to grasp their fate; if they do not, it is their fault rather than that of the stars. Free will is not simply conceded, but stressed – in *All's Well that Ends Well*, for instance:

> Our remedies oft in themselves do lie,
> Which we ascribe to heaven. The fated sky
> Gives us free scope; only doth backward pull
> Our slow designs when we ourselves are dull.

And finally, if there are still doubts, Shakespeare surely reveals his own feelings on the subject in the fourteenth sonnet:

> Not from the stars do I my judgement pluck,
> And yet methinks I have astronomy;
> But not to tell of good or evil luck,
> Of plagues, of dearths, or seasons' quality;
> Nor can I fortune to brief minutes tell,
> Pointing to each his thunder, rain and wind,
> Or say with princes if it shall go well
> By oft predict that I in heaven find . . .

Simon Forman, a prominent Elizabethan astrologer, much consulted by people at every level of society, whose journal reveals not only the extent of his practice but the enormous sexual success he enjoyed with his female clients

That is, astrology is to be used sensibly and realistically.

Some people, of course, were more credulous, among them Shakespeare's landlady Mrs Mountjoy, who went off from the house in Silver Street at least twice to consult an astrologer far inferior to John Dee, but more successful in his own line: Simon Forman (1552–1611).

Forman was, like so many astrologers of his time, a self-educated man who had picked up a knowledge of the subject with his knowledge of medicine – and throughout his life he was to be plagued by the Privy Council and the Royal College of Physicians for his unlicensed activities

OPPOSITE Tycho Brahe in Uraniborg, his observatory on the island of Hven (Ven), built and equipped for the greatest astronomer of his day by Frederick II of Denmark

LEFT In 1597, one Emilia Lanier consulted the astrologer Simon Forman about the career of her husband, a musician. Forman drew up his charts, advised her, and then (as usual with him) seduced her. The English historian A. L. Rowse is confident that Emilia Lanier was also the mistress of another Elizabethan, William Shakespeare; was, in fact, the 'Dark Lady' of the sonnets

EFFIGIES TYCHONIS BRAHE O. F.
ÆDIFICII ET INSTRUMENTORVM
ASTRONOMICORVM STRVCTORIS
AᵒᴼDOMINI 1587 ÆTATIS SVÆ 40

OPPOSITE The court astrologer of the Duke of Ferrara advised the artist Francesco del Cossa when, in 1470, he painted his frescoes of the months in the Palazzo di Schifanoia there. ABOVE *March*, a girl representing Spring hovers over Aries while Venus arrives in her swan-drawn chariot; (BELOW) *April* a youth holding the key of Spring is seated above Taurus, while Mars rides his chariot onto the scene

as an amateur doctor. Nevertheless (partly due to his courage in remaining in London to treat the sick during the plague) he built up a trustful clientele, and made a good living as a physician-astrologer.

His diaries and casebooks (detailed in A. L. Rowse's *Simon Forman*, 1974) reveal a cross-section of Elizabethan life, from the servant classes (though there are few of the poor, who could not afford his fees) to the famous, to wealthy merchants, politicians and the gentry – among them Frances Howard, Countess of Essex and Somerset. Among other things, his diaries are a record of his voracious love-life – he seems to have seduced most of his female clients, although the ease with which they fell to him is surprising to anyone who looks at the single surviving portrait.

The varied nature of the problems brought to Forman show the use ordinary people made of astrology: merchants asked about the prospects for coming voyages, while ship insurers asked about the possible perils into which the ships might run. Men came to enquire whether other men were their enemies or friends; women whether their love would be returned, whether they would become pregnant, whether they would ever marry. There were enquiries about missing pets, stolen goods; who had taken this piece of silver or that purse, and where was it hidden? There is truly no area of human life about which any kind of question might be asked, on which Forman was not consulted; in him, and in his successor William Lilly, astrology reaches its nadir of absurdity, in some senses – the silliest questions were deemed matters susceptible to the effects of the planets.

In the rest of Europe during the second half of the 16th century, there was a continued effort – especially in Germany – to put it on a serious scientific footing by collecting and collating notes on planetary positions and their apparent significance. John Garcaeus (1530–75) published four hundred birth charts of important contemporaries, a quarter of them prominent men of learning, so that they could be compared and discussed.

As usual, there are some dramatic stories. Valentin Nabod, Professor of Mathematics at Cologne, for instance, produced an interesting commentary on Ptolemy, but looking at his own birth chart believed himself to be in danger from a sword. He rented a house in Padua, whence he had travelled, and locked himself in it with a supply of food. The landlord, unable to collect the rent, had the door broken down after a while – and found the body of Nabod, stabbed to death.

That kind of story, quickly circulated by other astrologers, may have done something to convince the ignorant of the efficiency of astrological prediction. A more serious attempt was made in 1580, when Henry Ranzovius published his *Catalogue of Emperors, Kings and Princes who have loved, adorned and practised the art of astrology.* This contains many accounts of astrologers' successes by Manilius Antonius, chamberlain to Popes Sixtus IV and Julius II, Dethlevus Reventlovius, who worked for Charles V and successfully predicted the outcome of his war against the Elector of Saxony, Matthaeus Delius, who predicted to Philip II of Spain the diminution of his power after his succession. There were also, however, many apparently successful predictions included which were demonstrably inventions, which gave welcome ammunition to those who were beginning to claim that astrologers were given to cooking the books.

In England, popular and to some extent scientific interest in astrology was to continue to flourish throughout most of the 17th century; but by the close of the 16th century in the rest of Europe long shadows were closing in, not only over the quacks but over the genuine practitioners. The reasons for the gradual diminution of serious interest in astrology are various. Certainly the changing nature of man's understanding of the universe played its part. The almost universal realization that the Sun rather than the Earth was at the centre of the solar system seemed somehow to devalue the whole idea of astrology (although Newton was among those who realized that, since astrological influences – if they existed – were to be measured by noting the *relationships* between the planets, it was entirely possible to continue to respect the idea whatever body was at the centre of the system).

More important, probably, was the fact that the vast distance between the planets (to say nothing of the stars) was now recognized; it seemed extremely unlikely that any 'influence' (of whatever sort) could make itself felt at such a vast remove. Then there was the growing feeling that any 'scientific' idea should be capable of technical explanation; it was no longer enough to make the pronouncement 'This is so'. And finally, the temperament of scientists was on the change; the Age of Enlightenment was to reject, quite understandably, a 'science' which had gathered around it encrustations of magical and patently loony ideas such as that a birth chart could reveal the marital prospects of its subject's brother; that another could detail a previous incarnation; that a reliable answer to any question could be given by drawing up a chart for the moment of time when the question was asked.

The tide began to turn as early as the 1560s, when after a succession of Popes who were on the whole rather sympathetic to the occult there suddenly came a number who were both temperamentally and politically averse to it. Julius II and Adrian VI, during the first half of the 16th century, encouraged the Inquisition to act against 'magicians' – though at the same time Julius ordered an astrologer to elect an auspicious time at which the foundation stone of the Castle of Galliera should be laid, and his own statue erected at Bologna. Pius IV, in a papal bull of 1562, authorized action against various kinds of heretic, including those who pretended to be able to foretell the future by *sortilege* (casting lots). Gregory XIII, in 1581, ordered the Inquisition to act against those Jews who invoked the aid of demons for the same purpose.

Astrology was not mentioned specifically in any of these orders or exhortations, although Cardinal Francesco Albizzi spoke of it in 1566 as 'the most frequent means of divination', and therefore one for which the practitioners should be made to do penance, and exiled.

In 1586 things took a positive turn for the worse, when Sixtus V, elected to the papal chair on the death of Gregory XIII (not unsympathetic to astrology), enacted a bull against those practising judicial astrology, or even possessing books on the subject. God alone, the bull states, knows the future, and not even demons can foresee it – though to foretell the weather, natural disasters, the success or failure of crops, of voyages, or

A Commission works on the reformation of the calendar, in 1582, under the aegis of Pope Gregory XIII, who issued a bull cancelling ten days from the year, and instituted the 'new style' Gregorian calendar eventually accepted throughout Europe

to use astrology in medicine, is entirely proper. The casting of horoscopes, however, is not, and indeed God has seen to it that every separate soul has an angel whose duty is to protect it against the influence of the stars (so Sixtus obviously believed that the stars had some powers).

Astrologers were little daunted, unless they lived right under the eye of the Pope. Annual almanacs predicting the weather, and giving favourable days for bleeding or for planting seeds or whatever, continued to be published, and though astrology now ceased to be taught at the University of Bologna, it was to continue in the lecture rooms of other universities for many years. Salamanca is a good example: Gabriel Serrano taught astrology there between 1592 and 1598; Bartolomé de Valle was professor of astrology from 1612 until 1615, Francesco Reales (a priest) from 1615 to 1624, Núñez de Zamora from 1624 until 1640, Sanchez de Mendoza from 1647 to 1673, and but for a short break between 1706 and 1726 the chair was occupied continually until 1770.

This indicates that the Spanish Inquisition was not specially concerned to act against astrology, whatever the Pope said. And in fact astrology did not entirely vanish even from the Vatican, for in 1618 an astrologer addressed one of the resident cardinals, and Sixtus himself accepted the dedication of a series of books by Ionnes Paulus Gallicius of Salo on the nature and qualities of the planets, the radiation by which they exerted their influences from certain positions in the zodiac, arguing that in medicine it was absolutely necessary to use a chart in order properly to treat the patient. However, the publication of the more speculative almanacs certainly fell off in Italy, though elsewhere in Europe it continued unabated – sometimes as the result of Italian astrologers sending copy surreptitiously to printers in other countries; Rizza Casa, for instance, published predictions for the years 1586-90 at Lyons, in French.

From now on the Popes remained broadly unsympathetic, at least in public and at least to astrologers who claimed to be able to predict the future. In 1631 Urban VIII reaffirmed Sixtus' bull, threatening confiscation of property and even death to anyone who ignored it. He particularly disapproved of forecasts in politics and religion, and was just as antipathetic to the prediction of events in the lives of Popes and their relations as certain Roman Emperors had been to forecasts of their own downfall.

Astrologers did their best to fight back. Petrus Antonius de Magistris Galathei (1614-75) published a treatise arguing that the bull of Sixtus V had actually been directed only against superstitious astrologers, and that there were certainly areas of astrology that should be permitted to flourish. This was so; but a combination of the temper of the time and serious reconsideration of the basis of astrology made it more difficult for young students to accept old ideas, and even sometimes forced those formerly devoted to astrology to reassess their position.

Tommaso Campanella (1568-1639) is a case in point. This considerable Renaissance philosopher repeatedly asserted his acceptance of astrology, and even went so far, during his long imprisonment for plotting to free Naples from Spanish tyranny, as to write to Pope Paul V asserting that he was prejudiced against him for astrological reasons! Many other astrological allusions, arguments and predictions issued from his prison cell. He wrote six or seven books on astrology, asserting that the influences of the planets were physical, and that astrology was therefore a proper subject for the most religious scientific man to study.

He also, rather rashly, disputed the bulls of Sixtus and Urban, arguing that religion should not prohibit proper scientific experiment and discussion, that certainly astrologers should not be treated more harshly than heretics, and that it was quite improper to prohibit not merely forecasts of future events but even suggestions that this or that *might* happen – proper conjecture, in other words. However, in the end Campanella agreed that a papal bull, as such, was a papal bull, and should be obeyed, and even went so far as to agree that astrology was not in any real sense a science – though none the less susceptible of scientific study.

Such publications as the *Apologia* in which Campanella recanted his former opinions did nothing to bolster astrology's reputation against the mounting opposition. This was chiefly directed against the fiercer idiocies of the subject; still, no one denied that the Sun, Moon and planets had an effect on terrestrial matters, and even on men's lives and characters. But more and more it was disputed that there could be any prediction on the basis of planetary positions and movements. Some of the polemics directed against astrologers were not only intensely argued but argued at length. Alexander de Angelis, of Spoleto, head of the Jesuit College at Rome, published in 1615 no fewer than five books against astrology. It cannot be said that new astronomical knowledge actually added a great deal to the force of his arguments, which on the whole were yet again rehashings of old ones; the added force came from a new temperamental attitude rather than anything else – an attitude affecting scholars and scientists rather than the man in the street.

X

TOWARDS THE DARK

FOR centuries, the man in the street, *bourgeois* as well as relatively poor, had consulted astrologers when he could afford their fees; but more often he relied on the annual astrological almanacs which, for a relatively negligible sum of money, offered all sorts of help and advice.

Almanacs began as simple records of astronomical events during the coming year: notes of market days, holidays and holy days as well as of days when eclipses would occur, on which the Moon was full or new, on which notable celestial events such as conjunctions of the planets took place. In the Middle Ages these circulated in manuscript, or as 'clog almanacs' made of wood, metal or horn, with notches and symbols recording the lunar months and the church feast days. These were sometimes small enough to fit into a pocket, but occasionally more elaborate and even decorative, hanging on a nail at the fireside.

After the invention of printing almanacs were among the earliest books to be published: a printed almanac was issued by Gutenberg in 1448 – eight years before his famous Bible – and within thirty years a large number of them was being published, not only containing astronomical facts but predictions based on them. The earliest printed 'prognostication' to have survived is dated 1470, but within a few years others appeared printed in Germany, France, Italy, Hungary, the Netherlands and Poland. The first English almanac we have is dated 1500, printed by William Parron, an Italian who for a while attended the court of Henry VII, but vanished shortly after the death of the Queen at the age of 37.

While there is public rejoicing in the streets and the newly born Timur is presented to his mother, astrologers busily consult their reference books to draw up his horoscope

Din bon Jour de bon Cœur ma Comere Marguite.
Bonne vie et bon an Nicolle au gros Couquiau.
Aaa veft Agnes et Janne Mine frite.
He bée et barbe itou auec fon gros Muriau.
Cramique iauons tretoutes la lune fur la teste.
Buuons et Rigollons puisquil est nre feste.

En l'Imprimerie des
Nouueaux Caracthere
de Morau Rue St
Germain de laucerois
pres la Vallee de mifere
à Paris

Haye valentin dict barbe que faict don la notre homme.
Il cherche de la lune vn morceau qui est chu.
Car fil la peut trouuer il aura bonne fomme
Mais il ne voit pas Clair il a vn peu trop bu.
Lucas en est auffi et font tous deux si beftes.
Quon ne leur peut montrer quilz font deffus noz teste.

Manuscript almanacs continued to circulate for a long time after the invention of printing, and some 'clog almanacs' were still in use at the end of the 16th century. But printed copies were more common considerably earlier, many of them imported from the Continent, and containing weather forecasts, predictions of a good or bad harvest, notes of 'good' or 'evil' days, and even suggestions of the future prices of cereals, fruit and other crops.

Political predictions crept in, too – an interest in the doings of royalty seemed as common among early almanac readers as with readers of 20th-century gossip columns. The Laet family, which produced generations of Flemish astrologers whose almanacs were published at Antwerp, seems to have made a speciality of these, on one occasion predicting (for 1517) that Henry VIII of England would be inclined 'to pass the time in honour among fair ladies', and later promising that he would experience matrimonial difficulties.

The almanacs sold like hot cakes at every social level. Though the

The connection between the phases of the Moon and the female cycle, and between lunar activity and insanity, has been made for centuries, as in this 17th-century illustration depicting *L'influence de la lune sur la teste des femmes* nobility and gentry could well afford their own astrologers if they wished (and many of them did wish), they also bought the annuals, just as people today buy do-it-yourself health books to read in their doctors' waiting rooms. There is an almanac of 1624 with the autograph of Charles I inside the cover; Lord Burghley, Elizabeth's Treasurer, had a series in his library, some annotated in his own hand; Essex, the Parliamentary general, the Earl of Clarendon, Bishop Wren of Norwich were other subscribers – the last two making careful notes in their almanacs while imprisoned in the Tower of London. Many university dons 'took in' the almanacs, and seamen were devoted to them: Lieutenant John Weale, serving under Admiral Blake, took on his voyages 'a bottle of ink, a pocket almanac, and a sheet almanac'. As late as 1709 the Quakers of Derbyshire acquired (for a penny ha'penny) an almanac for their lending library.

Their popularity was enormous, partly because they were useful (as diaries, for instance), partly as popular entertainment. Some of them offered educational supplements on religion, medicine, magic, even sex: when the planets were in certain positions, love-making was positively dangerous – the 'dog days' of July and August were especially so. One satirist suggested that this was a time of year when adultery was common, for most husbands obeyed the astrologers' injunction to refrain from sex, and their wives turned to other quarters for satisfaction, on the grounds that 'if husband won't another must'. But there was positive advice, too: Walter Gray, in his notes for May 1581, simply enjoined 'Let Venus be embraced', while a contemporary suggested that his readers should 'embrace Venus honestly' in May, and 'daintily' in November. There is some evidence from population studies that people took this advice.

Dorothy Partridge, a midwife who with Sarah Jinner was one of a very few women astrologers, was more outright a century later: in January, she found 'a lusty squab bedfellow very good physic at this season'; but December and February were lusty months too, and an especially good time to be 'a husband to thy wife' was when the Moon was in Sagittarius.

The first Englishman to flood the market with his almanacs was William Lilly (1602-81), a yeoman's son from a tiny village in Leicestershire, who went to London as servant to an illiterate alderman and, marrying his rich widow, learned astrology from a disreputable master. By 1635 he was both teaching and practising astrology. It was in 1644 that as Merlinus Anglicus Junior he published his first almanac, and the publication continued annually until 1682, the year after his death. Lilly's notebooks are, like Forman's, a picture of an age, revealing the amount of work he did for men and women of all classes (he was consulted by

Charles I as well as by servants, by army generals, sea captains and rich merchants, and nonentities).

If Lilly was perhaps the best-known astrologer of the 17th century, there were others almost as notorious. (There were none whose forecasts were so well publicized: Lilly was actually arrested on a charge of starting the Great Fire of London, on the grounds that his alleged prediction of it was so accurate that he *must* have started it to justify himself!) John Booker (1603–67) was a haberdasher's apprentice before he became an astrologer; he published his own almanacs from 1631 to 1667, and recorded in his casebooks a thousand clients a year before 1648 and 1665. Lilly, better-known especially after the publication of his textbook *Christian Astrology* (1647), dealt with almost two thousand enquiries a year at the height of his activity. And they had two hundred or so colleagues between the reigns of Elizabeth and Anne.

ABOVE LEFT Sarah Jinner, one of the few women astrologers of the 17th century, published her almanacs between 1658 and 1664

ABOVE RIGHT Lilly's almanacs, bestsellers in his lifetime, contained many illustrations which were symbolic prognostications: in *Monarchy or no Monarchy* (1651) this woodcut suggested that a great fire would consume a city

Some of them were, to say the least, less respectable than Lilly or Booker, or even the rascally Forman. There was, for instance, one Captain Bubb, 'a proper handsome man, well spoken, but withal covetous', who stood in the pillory for fraud; Jeffery Neve, former alderman of Great Yarmouth and in 1626 deputy water-bailiff for Dover, who made a small fortune by rigging the accounts of the archery butts, and fled to Frankfurt; William Poole, 'a nibbler at astrology', who boasted that he had had seventeen professions, among them plasterer and bricklayer, and famous for the squib he published on Sir Thomas Jay, JP, who had falsely accused him of theft: on hearing of his death and burial, Poole made his way to the churchyard and defecated on the grave, leaving the following short note:

> Here lieth buried Sir Thomas Jay, Knight,
> Who being dead, I upon his grave did shite.

But there were many more respectable astrologers, of course, some from the ranks of the clergy. John Aubrey tells us that the knees of Richard Napier (1590-1674), rector of Great Linford in Buckinghamshire, were 'horny with praying', for he would go down on them before beginning to draw up each horoscope. He also plied his brethren with 'whole cloak-bags of books', converting many of them to astrology – including his neighbour the Rev. William Bredon, vicar of Thornton (so addicted to smoking, Lilly says, that when he had no tobacco he would cut the bellropes and smoke them). Then there were Anthony Asham, Richard Harvey, Thomas Buckminster, John Maplet, Stephen Batman and George Hartgill – all 16th-century clergymen astrologers – and, in the 17th century, Joshua Childrey, Nathaniel Sparke, John Butler, Edmund Chilmead, Charles Atkinson and Richard Carpenter (author of *Astrology proved harmless, useful and pious*, 1657).

Their advice, in and out of almanacs, remained as broad as that of their predecessors. During the Civil War, of course, the anxiety of parents for their fighting children, brother for brother, wife for husband, all increased their work load – and their incomes, when they were professionals; in 1662 it was said that Lilly was making £500 a year (at least £20,000 in today's currency). But it is difficult to estimate the average income of a professional astrologer: in 1647 Lilly received twenty pieces of gold for advising Charles I, but he and Booker would give individual astrological advice for two shillings and sixpence (12½p); Richard Delahay left between two and three thousand pounds at his death, but John Vaux, the clerk to St Helen's church, Auckland (who used to sell his almanacs from the altar) charged only one shilling for finding a stolen mare, or four shillings for a horse and a mare – with an additional eightpence to be spent on drink.

There has not yet been sufficient study of the part played by astrologers during the English Civil War. Not only did rival astrologers publish rival almanacs, and pay personal visits to the opposing Royalist or Parliamentary troops, but the newspapers published rival predictions of success and failure. Lilly had a great stroke of luck when early in the war, in 1645, he successfully predicted the Roundhead victory at Naseby; this success made his reputation. But he was roundly attacked by his rivals – on the Parliamentary side as well as the Royalist; for although he gave his support to Cromwell (and even worked for a while for the Commonwealth Council of State) he also advised Charles I, even procuring the file with which the king hoped to escape from Carisbrooke Castle! The war of the almanacs was long and bitter, with Lilly and Booker on one side, John Humphrey and George Wharton on the other. At one moment, indeed, Lilly and Booker were outside the walls of Colchester with the Parliamentary troops 'assuring them the town would very shortly be surrendered, as indeed it was', while Humphrey was inside the city advising the then governor, Sir Charles Lucas, that relief would soon reach him.

During the Interregnum before the restoration of the monarchy in 1660, the publication of almanacs continued, but there was some censorship, and some astrologers were executed for their support for the king, although Lilly managed to save Wharton, whose work he respected. Even Lilly himself was censored, while some colleagues had their publications stopped completely, and others were imprisoned. Unable to publish, they turned their attention to translating astrological classics hitherto unavailable in England, and this resulted in a great number of such works being available for the first time in English – added to which Lilly's rivals worked busily on textbooks to rival *Christian Astrology*, and Nicholas Culpepper, William Rameset, John Gadbury, Richard Saunders, John Partridge, William Salmon, and John Case all in time published popular guides to the subject.

The serious interest of intelligent men was slower to wane in England than abroad. It is true that as early as the 1560s a few men began to criticize the astrological theory as being scientifically unsound, at least where prediction was concerned. But the astrologers had their answer: they, or the majority of them, never claimed that anything in the future *would happen* – the most they would say was that some event, or some turn of health, or some change of fortune, seemed likely. In fact their almanacs were so crowded with 'maybe' and 'might' and 'perhaps' that they were criticized, as astrologers are today, of being too cagey. Yet all they were saying was that the stars compelled no man's action; all they did was to incline him one way or the other.

One section in the almanacs always read with interest concerned the weather: every almanac contained a section of weather forecasts, and readers seemed to find these useful. There were occasions on which the forecasts were extremely accurate. One famous example is that of *Patrick Murphy's Weather Almanac* for 1838. Against 20 January, Murphy noted: 'Fair. Prob. lowest degree of winter temperature.' That day proved in fact to be the coldest day not only of the year but of the century, the temperature falling to -20°F at Greenwich.

Astrologers mostly based their predictions on the movements of the Moon, which was believed to control the Earth's atmosphere. In France, Jean Baptiste Lamarck published his *Annuaire Météorologique* between 1800 and 1811, based on lunar data, and in Germany Rudolf Falb (1838–1903) coined the expression 'critical days' for dates when the Earth, Moon and Sun were in certain relative positions associated with various types of weather. In Russia, Demchinskii did similar work, publishing forecasts not only for his fatherland but for the United States and Japan. And for a moment to stretch even further into the future, the 20th-century descendants of Partridge and Gadbury and Lilly published their weather forecasts in *The Daily Mail* in England, and Demchinskii's long-term forecasts were also printed in that newspaper, and considered unusually accurate.

Astrometeorology has continued to flourish, and while professional meteorologists maintain a determinedly sceptical attitude, many of them will concede that insufficient study has been made of the planetary positions and their relationship to terrestrial weather. They might well do so, in the face of such evidence of success as that presented by the career of John Nelson, an American astrologer who between 1946 and 1971 investigated radio disturbances for the RCA network, and of 1500 forecasts made in 1967 (often months in advance) achieved a success rate of 93.2% – a rate maintained for nine years! Meteorologists are, at the time of publication, at last beginning to look seriously at the possibility that climatic cycles are linked to the movements of the so-called solar planets Mercury, Venus and Jupiter; there is, it is said, clear-cut evidence of associations between the period of peak solar tides and sunspot activity, and a link between sunspot activity, cosmic ray bombardment of Earth, and climatic change resulting from that bombardment.

But to return to the 17th century, it was not until the 1650s that general opinion in England began to swing against astrology. During Lilly's lifetime he and Wharton had been ridiculed by Samuel Butler in *Hudibras*, as Sidrophel and Whackham:

> *Some calculate the hidden fates*
> *Of monkeys, puppy-dogs and cats,*
> *Some running-nags and fighting-cocks;*
> *Some love, trade, law-suits, and the pox;*
> *Some take a measure of the lives*
> *Of Fathers, Mothers, Husbands, Wives,*
> *Make opposition, trine and quartile,*
> *Tell who is barren, and who fertile,*
> *As if the planet's first aspect*
> *The tender infant did infect*
> *In soul and body, and instill*
> *All future good, all future ill . . .*

There were less literary attacks, too, such as the squib put about which told of a country bumpkin who went to see Lilly about a stolen purse, and found the doorstep fouled with human excreta:

Down came that profound Ass-trologer . . . who opening the door and seeing it in that shitten case, began to execrate and curse those beastly knaves that did it; vowing that if he did but know who did him that nasty trick, he would make them examples to all such rogues so long as they lived. 'Nay,' quoth the countryman, 'if he cannot tell who beshit his door, he can as well be hanged as tell me who had my purse!' and so went his way.

Congreve sent up astrology, in the person of Foresign, in *Love for Love* (1695) – unlike Dryden, who thoroughly approved of it – and finally in came Swift with his demolition of the astrologer John Partridge in his *Predictions of Isaac Bickerstaff for 1708*.

In this fake almanac, Swift produced a straight-faced lampoon protesting that his real aim was to protect the public from the false claims of bad astrologers, and among other things predicted that Partridge himself would die at 11 p.m. on 29 March 1708, closely followed by King Louis XIV and the Pope. Shortly after 29 March, Swift published a detailed account of Partridge's sad death, and the latter had a hard struggle to prove himself still alive.

It is perhaps worth noting that neither Butler nor Swift (nor indeed any other writer who published anti-astrological work) actually set about destroying astrology by argument; all they did was ridicule it – and goodness knows it presented a broad enough target. Sometimes they did so for political reasons; as a matter of fact this was probably the case with Swift, for Partridge was a vociferous Whig and republican.

New argument about the basis of astrology was, as always, lacking. It was certainly not provided by the astronomers. It has been suggested that Newton was almost personally responsible for the desuetude of astrology in England. Nothing could be further from the truth. His work may have made its contribution to the changing climate of opinion, but he clung to a belief in astrology until his death, and was very short with Edmund Halley when, as we have seen, the latter rebuked him for heeding such nonsense: 'Sir,' he said, 'I have studied the matter – you have not.'

Nevertheless, the temper of the time was against him. Doubts were openly expressed at the universities, and for the first time the use of astrology in medicine was questioned. The Royal College of Physicians turned against it, despite the fact that its President between 1601 and 1604 was an almanac writer and there was some use of astrology in the College's *Pharmacopoeia*. Those attacked were (yet again) the extremists. No one rebuked Richard Mead, a vice-president of the Royal Society, for publishing in 1717 *A treatise concerning the influence of the Sun and Moon upon human bodies*, and arguing that attacks of epilepsy, vertigo, hysteria and asthma could be collated with phases of the Moon; and in 1680 it was claimed that astrological physicians were the most popular and sought-after of all doctors. John Locke, who has been called the inspirer of the Age of Enlightenment, and whose philosophy had the most profound influence on the thought of Europe, accepted that the curative value of herbs was enhanced by their being picked and used at particular times of the year.

Still, by the turn of the century scientific interest in astrology was at its lowest ebb for many hundreds of years indeed, perhaps since the 3rd or 4th centuries BC. Although there had still been no concerted attack on the theory from astronomers or universities, it was now the case that the former were no longer automatically interested in the effects the heavenly bodies had on earth; it was simply assumed that, apart from the obvious effects of Sun and Moon, they had none. The intellectual aspects of the subject, the philosophical and theological implications, were on the whole no longer discussed except by a decreasing minority.

By 1720 the last of the notable astrologers of the 17th century was dead – Francis Moore died in 1714, John Partridge in the following year – and with them a generation which, whatever its faults, had taken astrology seriously and practised it with some pretension to scholarship. Lilly's *Christian Astrology*, for instance, is an immensely long work (something like 350,000 words in three volumes) enshrining much traditional astrology culled from a long check list of earlier volumes, some at that time untranslated. Whatever may be one's opinion of some of Lilly's wilder

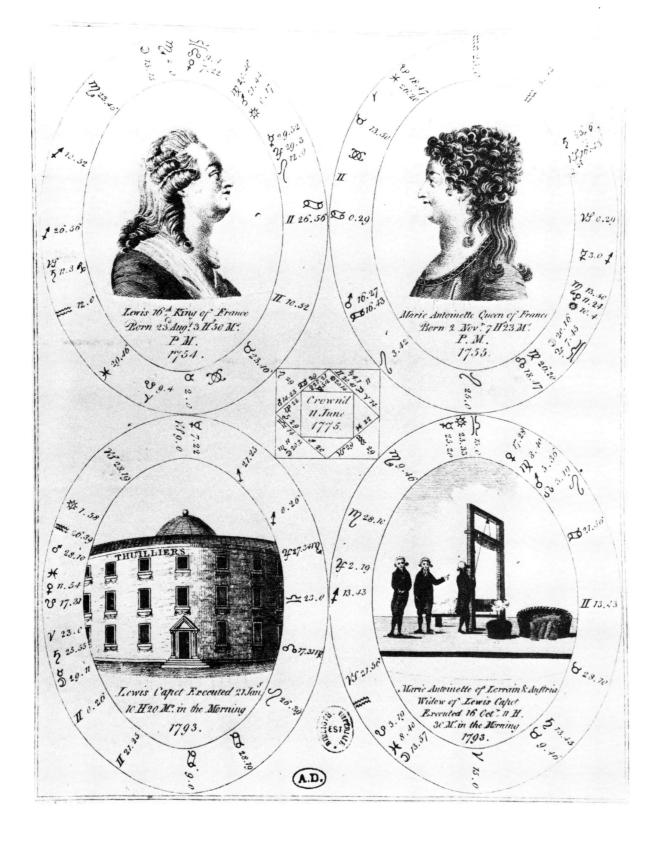

Lewis 16th King of France
Born 23 Augt 3 H 50 Mt.
P.M.
1754.

Marie Antoinette Queen of France
Born 2 Novr 7 H 23 Mt.
P.M.
1755.

Crown'd
11 June
1775.

Lewis Capet Executed 21 Jany
10 H 20 Mt. in the Morning
1793.

Marie Antoinette of Lorrain & Austria
Widow of Lewis Capet
Executed 16 Octr. 11 H.
30 Mt. in the Morning
1793.

THUILLIERS

assertions about what astrology can and cannot do, it is an intelligently written work. No 18th-century astrologer would have been capable of it; they were far less interested in the intellectual or empirical truth of the claims they made, and most often were simply not intelligent enough for the subject. They were, on the whole, cheapjacks.

There had been a few attempts to bring the study of astrology into line with the new scientific age: J. B. Morin's posthumous *Astrologia Gallica* (1661) argued that any serious study of astrology must depend on a systemic examination of meteorological, political and religious developments in relation to the movements of the planets, and that any other method of examining the subject did more harm than good. Joshua Childrey, an archdeacon of Salisbury, had argued for a reformation of astrology on the lines suggested by Francis Bacon, and Jeremy Shakerley, an astrologer much under Lilly's influence, wrote that 'astrology consists of too much uncertainty to inform us of anything', and was ambitious to seek 'from philosophical principles a foundation for a more refined astrology'. Even John Gadbury claimed that 'one real experiment is of greater worth and more to be valued than one hundred pompous predictions.'

But the 18th century set off on its course of scientific empiricism, and determined to ignore the efforts of astrologers to claim that their subject should be included among those to be examined in a similar fashion. The attitude continues to this day: one scientist at a conference in the 1970s, dissatisfied with statistical evidence offered as proof that some aspects of astrology were worth examination, was asked what kind of proof he *would* accept, and replied with splendid certainty: 'I can conceive of *no* evidence which would convince me that there is anything in the subject.'

If there were few serious astrologers in the 18th century, and even fewer in the 19th, there was plenty of money-making activity from quacks; the evidence of this lies in the continuing sale of almanacs. Partridge's annual almanacs continued to sell for over a century after his death, and *Old Moore's Almanac* is still issued in the 1980s. In 1764, *Old Moore* sold over 80,000 copies in a year, although its prophesies were even more general, even more garbled, than those of earlier issues.

One development during the 18th century was the appearance of almanacs directed specifically at women readers: *The Ladies' Diary*, for instance, which appeared in 1704, and had articles on famous women, recipes and riddles as well as astrological items. Its editor, a Coventry schoolmaster called John Tipper, had the ambition of 'introducing the fair sex to the study of mathematics'. By the 1750s, it was selling 30,000 copies a year, and was widely read by gentlemen.

Astrologers, for their own interest and that of their followers, naturally published charts of the planetary positions at the birth of important people, and of important events. Soon after the culmination of the French Revolution, charts were published for the births of Louis XVI and Queen Marie Antoinette, together with charts for the moments of their execution

Critics of astrology had their say in popular cartoons: here, astrologers observing the heavens are surrounded by admiring, foolish females, a professional fool, and a magician standing inside his magic circle and keeping a couple of enquiring devils in their places

Such astrologers as there were, were as fiercely partisan in politics as the earlier astrologers had been during the Civil War. George Parker was a high Tory whose views were so incendiary that the Stationers' Company refused to publish his work; Partridge on the other hand was violently Whig, and greeted the accession of George of Hanover as a day of deliverance from 'popery, slavery and English traitors'.

Towards the middle of the century, there was a swing towards religion, as though the astrologers wished to strengthen their position by getting the Creator on their side. They emphasized the fact that only God could have worked out so finely the intricate movements of the planets; and even the composition of the matter of which the earth and stars were made proved the existence of God. As Job Gadbury, John Gadbury's cousin, put it, there could be nothing in the recently advanced theories that atoms came together by chance to form the universe, for 'though the air we breathe be full of them, yet they tend to nothing but to make us wink.'

The everyday work of the consultant astrologers went on much as it had always done: advice was offered about illness, love, lost property, and so on. There seems to have been a sufficient popular interest for a large number of astrologers to make a reasonable professional living, although the fact that many of them are found rebuking members of the public who came to see them merely for amusement, and advising colleagues to get their hands on the fee before beginning to cast the horoscope, seems to indicate that a certain amount of doubt was now to be found at all levels of society and education.

The major British astrologer of the century seems to have been Henry Season (1693–1775), a doctor and surgeon from Wiltshire, who like most of the former astrologers was virtually self-educated, for he never attended school for more than six weeks at a time. He taught himself medicine and astrology, like Lilly and Forman, and after an apprenticeship during which he seems to have invented his own medicinal cures, managed to get a licence to practise as physician and surgeon.

The almanacs he published show him to be a very traditional sort of astrologer, giving the usual sort of advice; but he also used them for political argument, and as means of general advertisement of his personal views on everything under the sun – from the fact that stage plays were a disgraceful evil, to the view that it was a good thing man would never be able to visit the Moon, for he would without any doubt corrupt its inhabitants.

By the 1790s astrologers were numerous enough to have their own magazine, devoted entirely to 'a science which was studied by the patriarchs of the first ages, but which, by the craft of ignorance of pretenders, has been exposed to much calumny and error.' However, the magazine was ill supported (because much of it was devoted to non-astrological chatter about the occult) and ceased publication after its seventh issue.

Newspaper advertisements, scattered through the provincial press, indicate that astrologers still flourished, ready not only to give, on receipt of the date, time and place of birth, a 'true description of the complexion, colour of the hair, private marks and moles, temper &c', but (to quote John Worsdale of Lincolnshire) to help 'those persons afflicted with disorders of various denominations'. On receipt of the necessary details, 'the nature and origin of the disease may be truly ascertained, and a remedy prescribed for all curable disorders, by the ancient rules of elementary philosophy.'

In America, the situation was rather similar. Some attention was paid to the subject at the universities at the turn of the century. Charles Morton, who had been educated at Oxford during the English Civil War, and left the country in 1686 to become a Presbyterian minister at Charlestown, Massachusetts, had his *Compendium physicae* accepted at Harvard, where it formed the basis of the study of modern science. While forcefully denying the fortune-telling aspects of astrology,

The flying days and months are hurrying on,
Years press on years, impatient to be gone,
With eager steps to bring th' important hour,
When angry fires this system shall devour.

An engraving from an
early American almanac

THE ANATOMY of MAN's BODY, as governed by the twelve CONSTELLATIONS, viz.

♈ governs the Head and Face.

♉ Neck.

♋ Breaſt

♍ Bowe.

♏ Secret.

♑ Knee..

♊ Arms.

♌ Heart.

♎ Reins.

♐ Thighs.

♒ Legs.

♓ The feet.

Aries ♈ a Ram.   Taurus ♉ a Bull.   Gemini ♊ Twins. Cancer ♋ a Crab Fiſh.   Leo ♌ Lion.   Virgo ♍ a Virgin.   Libra ♎ Balance, or Scales.   Scorpio ♏ a Scorpion. Sagittarius ♐ an Archer. Capricornus ♑ a Goat.   Aquarius ♒ a Young Man pouring water out of a pot.   Pisces ♓ a Fiſh.

TO know where the Sign is, find the Day of the Month, and againſt the Day in the 6th Column, you have the Sign or Place of the Moon, and the Part of the Body it governs.

The Names and Characters of the Seven PLANETS

♄ Saturn, ♃ Jupiter, ♂ Mars, ☉ Sol, ♀ Venus, ☿ Mercury, ☽ Luna.

The 'astrological man' continued to appear, as here, in an 18th-century American almanac

Morton examined the connection between the planets and meteorology, and the influence of their movements on the human body and mind.

> On the whole matter [he concluded], I judge that as to weather and temperatures of our bodies with relations to health or sickness by good observations of prudent and philosophical minds, a useful knowledge might be framed; but for all the rest that is pretended the books written about them might make a curious bonfire according to the primitive pattern ...

Other Harvard men showed some interest: for instance Samuel Willard, its vice-president between 1701 and 1707, and John Leverett, his successor. Willard pointed out that 'astrologers have had their predictions, that do sometimes fall out right' (a cautious approbation, if approbation it was). Isaac Greenwood, Harvard's first Hollis Professor of Mathematics and Natural Philosophy, replaced Morton's *Compendium* in 1728 with his own *Philosophical discourse concerning the mutability and change of the natural world*, in which, disapproving of judicial astrology, he nevertheless asserted that

> tides are produced in the ocean, winds in the atmosphere, many changes in inanimate and animate bodies, and in the human economy itself. Astrology seems to have a philosophical foundation, and we know not how many wonders and mysteries may be the genuine effects of this great alternative in nature.

Through the 18th century Harvard took this cautiously positive attitude, accepting in 1762 a master's thesis which argued that 'the heavenly bodies produce certain changes in the bodies of animals', and publicly asserting that the time was speedily coming when Virginia would 'surpass the Greeks in philosophy, the Egyptians in geometry, the Phoenicians in arithmetic, and Chaldeans in astrology.'

Yale was not behind Harvard in its toleration of astrological studies. Samuel Johnson, who graduated from that university in 1714 to become a Congregationalist minister, included an essay in his *Revised Encyclopaedia* of 1716 on 'The starry heavens and their power and influences for the subject of astrology', and though in 1718 a Yale thesis was arguing that 'all the predictions of the astrologers with regard to future contingent events are fallacious and vain', this was an attack on judicial rather than on 'natural' astrology.

As to educated opinion among non-academics, this may perhaps be deduced from an article in Chambers's *Cyclopaedia*, so commonly read, which also attacked judicial astrology as 'superstition', but left natural astrology unrebuked, although pointing out that it was 'only to be deduced, a posteriori, from phaenomena and observations.'

Those who did not have Chambers on their bookshelves certainly for the most part had an almanac or two; these were almost as common, and in much the same vein, as the English almanacs of the same period. But there was an additional emphasis on agriculture and meteorology. Culpepper was extremely popular, and as late as the middle of the 18th century the most common medical 'textbook' in the American home was his *London Dispensatory*. As time went on, this was attacked – in particular by Cotton Mather, the Congregational minister and author, who while splendidly gullible about such matters as angels and mermaids, had some kind of natural antipathy to astrology (mainly on religious grounds) and argued that to suppose that the efficacy of certain herbs was in any way enhanced by their being picked at certain times was 'a folly akin to the idolatry and superstition of the Roman-Catholics, in looking to saints, for their influences on our several diseases.'

American farmers in the 17th and 18th centuries seem to have paid special attention to astrological and veterinary advice: an almanac argued that 'for the better success in letting blood, taking physick, cutting of cattle, sheep and hogs, it's necessary to know where, or in what part of the body the sign is', and in *The Husbandman's Magazine* of 1718, John Smith set it down that horses should be gelded 'in the wain of the Moon, the signs being either in Virgo or Aries', and that 'Candlemas (observing it to be in the increase of the Moon) is the best time to let your sows be covered.'

The efficient American farmer must have lived his life entirely according to the zodiac and the planets, if we are to believe the magazines of the period; in 1712 *The Husbandman's Guide* advised its readers to 'geld sheep and other cattle the Moon being in Aries, Sagittarius or Capricorn. Sheer sheep the Moon increasing in Taurus, Virgo or Libra, and their fleeces will grow the thicker and faster, the like observed in cutting hair; and if the Moon be in a friendly aspect to Venus 'tis much better.' Fifty years later *The Citizen's and Countryman's Experienced Farrier* advised farmers who wanted 'to get horse colts' to 'take your mare to the horse before the full of the Moon, and when the sign is a female. To get mare colts, cover after the full, and in the male signs.'

There was horticultural advice too – (trees should be set and dug up in winter, 'especially at new Moon', fruit trees planted and grafted when the Moon was waxing, transplanted trees set when it was waning – for the waning Moon helped a plant send its root downwards, while the waxing Moon helped a plant to grow upward), and some personal ('it is good to bathe the Moon being in Taurus, Virgo and Capricorn; it is best bathing two or three days after, or at the full of the Moon').

OPPOSITE **William Lilly,** the most popular and best-known astrologer of 17th-century England, was consulted by most prominent Parliamentary commanders, though at the same time he was involved in a plot to enable Charles I to escape from imprisonment.

OVERLEAF LEFT Many illustrations of 'the planets and their influences' were published in the 18th century. These show the effects of Mercury and Venus. *Mercury*, (BELOW) has Mercury with the Gemini twins in the background: below him men engage in the Mercurial activities of scholarship and trade; a cock stands nearby, and in the background is a ship representing transport and communication. In the *Venus* picture (ABOVE) she is accompanied by Taurus and blind Cupid, and beneath her courtship, music and feasting are seen

OVERLEAF RIGHT By the middle of the 17th century, popular almanacs were already neglecting genuine astrology for fortune-telling; these three delightful 19th-century covers (THIRD OPPOSITE p. 169 ABOVE) show the connection with 'magic' in the portrayal of wizards, and of the ubiquitous Nostradamus

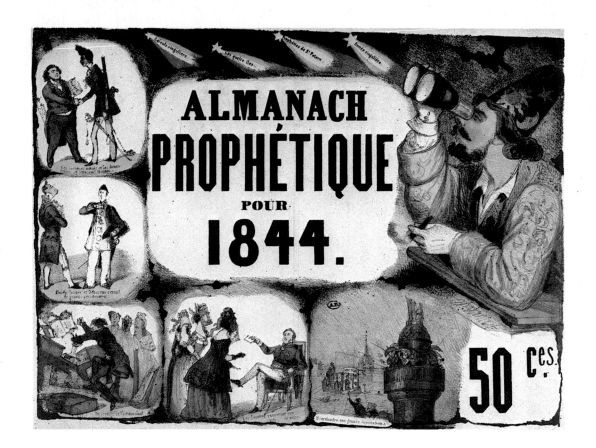

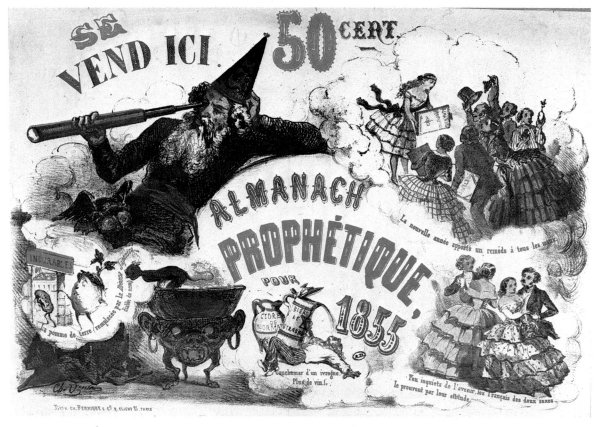

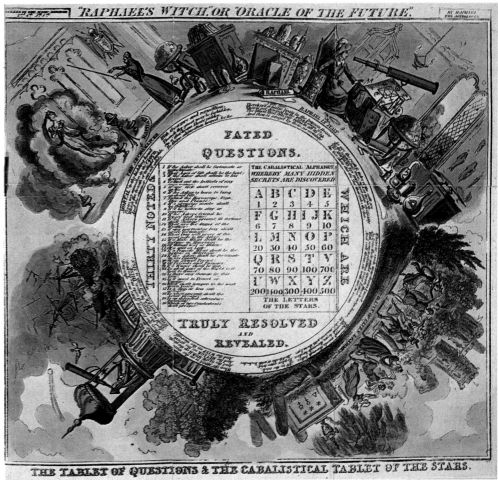

THE TABLET OF QUESTIONS & THE CABALISTICAL TABLET OF THE STARS.

OPPOSITE ABOVE (see p. 168) OPPOSITE BELOW
Raphael's Witch or Oracle of the Future, gives a list of *Fated Questions truly Resolved and Revealed* with the help of *The Cabalistic Alphabet, the Letters of the Stars*. The questions include 'Whether the asker shall attain to his desire', 'if the asker is born to long life', and 'if a wager shall be won'

There was opposition, of course, from those who found it ludicrous that 'in many parts of the country ... a citizen will not castrate a lamb or a pig, nor suffer himself nor any of his family to be bled from the arm, without inspecting the almanac in the first place, to find what the philomath who compiled it has certified for the astral and lunar influence on the body for that day.' But there was some serious study, too; in 1764 a Dr James Greenhill was correlating the fits experienced by an epileptic slave with the changes of the Moon, and a number of other doctors had received astrological training and used it in treating their patients. Samuel Deane, a respected agriculturist, published his theory on the effects of the planets on fruit-tree growth in *The New England Farmer, or Georgic Dictionary* (1797):

Some may think it whimsical to gather apples on the day of the full Moon. But, as we know both animals and vegetables are influenced by the Moon in some cases, why may we not suppose a greater quantity of spirit is sent up into the fruit, when the attraction of the heavenly bodies is greatest? If so, I gather my apples at the time of their greatest perfection, when they have most in them that tends to their preservation ...

There were a few consultant astrologers practising in America at this time: Joseph Stafford of Rhode Island, Nathaniel Low of Boston, John Jarman, Nathaniel Ames and Daniel Leeds of Philadelphia, John Tobler of North Carolina. Low and Ames were rivals in the first half of the 18th century, Ames claiming to have foretold the death of George II and the victories of George III's forces in the French and Indian war, while Low warned, on the eve of the French and American revolutions, that certain planetary aspects 'may stir up great politicians in contriving new ways and methods of regulating the affairs of governments.' Eventually, the polymath Benjamin Franklin disposed of Leeds by emulating the prank played by Swift on Isaac Bickerstaff: he predicted Leeds's death, 'proved' it, and ran the poor man out of business despite all his protestations that he was still alive and well.

There is not much information about the practices of these American astrologers, but a contemporary diary reveals at least that on Rhode Island privateers were consulting astrologers about the time at which they should set sail (though two of them, advised to sail on Friday, 24 December, did so in the middle of a snowstorm and went down with all hands); merchants seem to have employed astrologers similarly – and even Franklin himself did so, on one occasion.

In general, although there were several different emphases, astrology in America (like much else) was broadly imitative of astrology in Britain;

there, as in the mother country, astrologers relied on the popularity of their almanacs to keep them afloat.

Since the earliest days of the printed almanac, it had been the case that the livelier an astrologer's pen was, the more success he had; Lilly's popular success was in a very large measure due to his pawky, roistering style. At the end of the 18th century, when natural scepticism made the simple provision of predictions unacceptable, it was even more important for astrologers to entertain their readers, and the tradition of the astrological journalist became much stronger – to reach its apogee a century and a half later, in the newspaper astrologer.

In the early part of the 19th century, the most popular almanac in Britain was the *Vox Stellarum*, which by 1839 was selling over half a million copies – rather surprising, perhaps, when one considers that it was editorially very much on the side of the Americans in the War of Independence, believing that the result 'paved the way for freedom', and positively welcomed the French Revolution with its 'glorious and happy spirit of liberty'. It did, however, take England's part in the war against France.

Enormous sales of almanacs, especially the cheaper ones, continued through the 19th century; in 1897 over a million copies of *Old Moore's Penny Almanac* were printed, and every one sold within two months of the end of the year (the predictions were, of course, for 1898). It was complained, halfway through the reign of Queen Victoria, that practically no one among the 'lower classes' did not possess an almanac, and most lived their lives by it, refusing to cut their grass if rain was predicted, declining to dose their cattle if the day was inauspicious.

Some of the credit, if that is the word, for the growing popularity of purely astrological magazines (combining the kind of predictions offered in the old-style almanacs with feature articles and gossip) must lie with two men, Robert Cross Smith and Richard James Morrison, both born in 1795. Smith was in 1824 appointed editor of a new periodical, *The Straggling Astrologer of the Nineteenth Century*, in the twelfth issue of which appeared for the first time his pseudonym 'Raphael', which was to become famous in the next few years. He also introduced a weekly feature predicting the planetary effects on love and marriage, finance, business, travel – the first weekly predictions to be made in a journal.

The Straggling Astrologer did not last long; Smith had better luck with *The Prophetic Messenger*, the first issue of which came out in 1826, and which on his death in 1832 was taken over and continued until 1858. There were at least five 'Raphaels' after Smith.

It was Morrison, however, who was the more important of the two men, working under the pseudonym 'Zadkiel'. An ex-naval officer, he became a professional astrologer in 1830 and founded *Zadkiel's Almanac*, sales of which rivalled those of *The Prophetic Messenger*. Apart from his journalism, Morrison did much to make astrology mildly respectable again. He complained, for instance, about the cheapjack astrologers who would work for as little as five shillings, when 'no man of education would stoop to receive such beggarly remuneration', and recommended that anyone wishing to consult an astrologer should go to one possessing the Diploma of the British Association for Astral Science (founded in 1844 with 107 members, but short-lived).

In his 1861 almanac, Morrison published a suggestion that Saturn's position during that year would be 'very evil for all persons born on or near the 26th August; among the sufferers I regret to see the worthy Prince Consort of these realms. Let such persons pay scrupulous attention to health.' On 14 December 1861, the Prince Consort died of typhoid.

Far from being congratulated on his accuracy, Zadkiel was consequently attacked by a leader writer in *The Daily Telegraph*, and forced to sue a rear-admiral who blackguarded him in the same newspaper. He won the case, evidence having been given for him by a large queue of titled clients; but the Lord Chief Justice was deeply unsympathetic, allowed continual laughter in court, and recommended low damages. Zadkiel received only twenty shillings and had to pay his own costs. The sales of his next almanac profited by the publicity, but as a consultant astrologer he almost vanishes from sight from that moment.

Morrison/Zadkiel could certainly not be disqualified from the accusation of having an interest in the occult – especially in crystal-gazing, an occupation which was really at the root of his libel case. But he was a serious astrologer too, preparing and publishing in 1852 a popular abridgement of Lilly's *Christian Astrology*; and there were others – such as William Joseph Simmonite, elected to the Council of the London Meteorological Society (of which Morrison was also a member), and Richard Garnett (1835–1906), on the staff of the British Museum, an amateur who impressed Samuel Butler with some predictive successes.

It was Garnett who, in an essay entitled *The Soul and the Stars*, published in *The University Magazine* in 1880, put forward a view of astrology which was at odds with that of many professional astrologers, still much caught up with almanacs and predictions. Garnett took the view that far from being an occult science, as most people thought, it was 'necessary to insist on the strictly empirical character of astrology', that 'astrology with the single exception of astronomy, is, as regards the certainty of its data, the most exact of all exact sciences', and that the

astrologer's calculations 'are performed by no more cabalistic process than arithmetic. The influence he attributes to the heavenly bodies may be imaginary, but in no sense occult ...'

Alan Leo, one of the best-known astrologers of his time, whose textbooks are still in print, and used by students of astrology

Garnett was looking towards our own time, when astrologers would for the most part share his view. Others, however, were to pave the way for the 20th-century resurgence of interest in the subject. Alan Leo (W. F. Allen, 1860–1917) was one.

Leo is an important figure in Western astrology, his textbooks still on sale. Through his friend 'Sepharial' (W. R. Old, 1864–1929) he found his way into Madame Blavatsky's Theosophical Society in London. He became a professional astrologer, and set up a sort of factory in Hampstead, where other astrologers were set to calculate charts, and several clerks to write out Leo's opinions on them; it was the Victorian equivalent of today's computerized horoscope firms, and Leo's Modern Astrology Publishing Company soon had branches in Paris and New York.

It was Leo's chief clerk who devised the system by which cheapjack astrologers still work: answer their advertisements in the best-selling astrological magazines, and you will receive a number of cyclostyled sheets stapled together, one for the Sun sign, one for the rising sign, one each for the positions of the Moon, Venus, Mercury and so on. E. H. Bailey, who cordially disliked him, later described an average morning in Lyncroft Gardens – one that has often been reproduced since:

The morning mail had just been delivered and Albanus Leon [Leo] was busily engaged in sorting out a large pile of letters of all shapes and sizes ... Most of

THE HIEROGLYPHIC FOR 1852.

Zadkiel's Almanac for 1852 included this hieroglyphic showing a wounded lion, an erupting volcano, vague insurrection in some foreign clime, and a despondent Britannia. It could be used (like Lilly's hieroglyphics before it) to illustrate any one of a multitude of possible disasters. What was made of the friar riding a bull is more obscure

them contained money orders, for Leon had an immense clientele, and the income from his business had now reached four figures a year, and bid fair to greatly increase as time went on. The mail this morning was an exceptionally heavy one and the pile of postal and money orders was rapidly mounting. It was true that the great majority were only for a shilling, but these, with the five and ten shillings orders, and three or four for a pound, as well as various cheques for various amounts, made up a very goodly sum.

'Raphael' and 'Zadkiel' were of that generation of astrologers faced with the problem of assimilating into the tradition the 'modern' planets Uranus (discovered in 1781) and Neptune (1846); Pluto was to be added in 1930. The discovery of these planets was another handy weapon for the anti-astrological camp – but astrologers replied that rather than creating new problems, they solved old ones. Looking at a horoscope of, say,

The astronomical observatory at Delhi, used for observations employed for astrological purposes, was built for the Emperor Muhammed Shah in about 1724. The *Misra-Yantra* (shown here) enabled astronomers to calculate the meridian at noon for four places, two in Europe, one in Japan and one in the Pacific, to establish meridian altitudes, and to calculate the precise time of the entry of the Sun into Cancer. The *Samrat-Yantra*, an enormous gnomen forming a triangle with the hypotenuse parallel to the Earth's axis, measures the time of day exact to within half a second, and also measures the declination of the Sun and other planets

Queen Elizabeth I or one of the Caesars, it was clear that there were some elements of the character which were not to be accounted for by the positions of the planets known to ancient astrologers. These were obviously the result of the influence of those planets recently discovered, and if they were filled into the old birth charts, the picture was much more complete.

Similarly, the effects of the 'new' planets in a progressed chart were slowly discovered by a process of trial and elimination. Harvey's discovery of the circulation of the blood had not devalued what was previously known about the bodily processes; it had simply enlarged that process. The same was true of the 'modern' planets.

INTO THE
TWENTIETH CENTURY

HILST Alan Leo took the lead in maintaining the popular interest in astrology in England, it was the great psychologist Carl Gustav Jung (1875–1961) who probably more than any other single person encouraged at least a few scientists to begin to think about the subject.

Jung's interest in astrology seems to have been a natural offshoot of his preoccupation with the 'collective unconscious', his belief that 'although our inheritance consists in physiological paths, still it was mental processes in our ancestors that created the paths'; that, in fact, 20th-century man's attitude to life is shaped by his remote history. Jung saw the signs of the zodiac as archetypal – that is, as having for us a significance deeper than we know; and we are conscious of archetypes when stirred by highly emotional circumstances, such as those that provoke people to consult astrologers.

Jung himself seems to have used the horoscope as a starting point from which to build a bridge of understanding between himself and a patient by finding within it and his own chart some common ground. During the preparation of his essay on *synchronicity* (the term he coined to explain the wild coincidences that occur in almost everyone's life, and can be not only puzzling but frightening) he and his assistants examined the birth charts of 180 apparently happily married couples, and sought in them the traditional astrological indications of satisfactory partnership. Later, he added more data, and eventually investigated the 966 charts of 483 couples, not only in their original pairings but in chance couplings – so altogether 32,220 pairings were postulated and examined.

Preis 10 Pf. = 15 Heller.

1915

1914

E.DS.

Das Ende des Weltkrieges,

wie es in den Sternen geschrieben steht.

(Das Horoskop des Weltkrieges)

Von einem Aftrologen.

Leipzig
Verlag von Siegbert Schnurpfeil.

During the First World War (as again during the Second) astrology was used for propaganda purposes

The results of the test were considered by Jung to be, in the end, somewhat unsatisfactory; but he did point out that in the twinned charts of the happily married couples there was a statistically significant presence of the aspects traditionally considered indicative of a satisfactory relationship. He expressed this very dramatically:

You take three matchboxes, put 1000 black ants in the first, 10,000 in the second and 50 in the third, together with one white ant in each of them, shut the boxes, and bore a hole in each of them, small enough to allow only one ant to crawl through at a time. The first ant to come out of each of the three boxes is always the white one.

The chances of this actually happening are extremely improbable. Even in the first two cases, the probability works out at 1:100 × 10,000, which means that such a coincidence is to be expected only in one case out of ten million. It is improbable that it would ever happen in anyone's experience. Yet in my statistical experiment it happened that precisely the three conjunctions stressed by astrological tradition came together in the most improbable way.

Jung was conscious of the statistical blemishes of his experiment, and never claimed that it proved anything other than that, in the words of J. S. Haldane, 'the universe may be not only queerer than we suppose, but queerer than we *can* suppose.' But his astrological essay (*Synchronicity, an acausal connecting principle*, 1955) had the effect of directing some serious minds towards the disreputable science, and it is during the past twenty years that interest, in particular, has steadily grown.

Before Jung's rather specialized interest took shape, isolated examples are to be found of a revival of serious attention to the subject. In 1891, in France, while popular interest was scant (and it was possible for a scientist to assert that astrology was an ancient science whose rules had been completely lost), a kind of cabalist astrology was revived, which led to the publication of a translation of part of Morin de Villefranche's *Astrologia Gallica* of 1661, which in turn interested an artillery officer called Paul Choisnard (1867–1930), who became the first modern astrologer to attempt to get together a reliable body of statistical evidence about the planet's influences on the human personality.

It was Madame Blavatsky who triggered off the renewal of interest in Germany, which spread largely as a result of the work of Karl Brandler-Pracht (born 1864), who seems to have learned astrology in the United States, where he worked as an actor. He founded the German Astrological Society, and started the *Astrologische Rundschau*, the most prominent astrological journal in Germany until the Nazis shut it down in 1938.

It was after the First World War, among the uncertainties of the peace, that astrology really began to gain ground in Germany, and the publication of ephemerides (tables of the positions of celestial bodies) and almanacs boomed. The best-known astrologer of the years between the wars was without doubt Elspeth Ebertin (born 1880), a serious astrologer with a genius for popular journalism, which she combined with consultancy. It was Frau Ebertin who, sent the birth data of Adolf Hitler in 1923, wrote in her yearbook that he 'could expose himself to danger by lack of caution' – which he duly did during the Munich *putsch*, when he fell and broke his shoulder before being arrested and imprisoned. Frau Ebertin received concommitant publicity.

Although the German police from time to time prosecuted individual astrologers for fortune-telling, interest grew, and annual conferences of astrologers were held between 1923 and 1936, only internecine rows hindering ambitious plans for scientific study. The Germans have the distinction of recognizing the putative importance of astrology in the developing art of psychoanalysis, and one of Jung's admirers, O. A. H. Schmitz (1873-1931) led the way in proposing how this could best be done, though Herbert Freiherr von Kloeckler (1896-1950) was the pioneer in dragging astroanalysis into the psychology-conscious 20th century, with his *Grundlagen für die astrologische Deutung* (*Foundations of astrological interpretation*), 1926.

Interest in astrology being as intense, in Germany, as it was – Ellic Howe, in *Urania's children*, 1967, estimates that during the twenty years after 1921 at least four hundred specialist books and pamphlets were published in that country – it was inevitable that it should be suspected that Hitler and the Nazi party made use of astrology for their own purposes. As with other homogenous groups, some astrologers supported the Nazis, some did not; on both sides, there were unhappy consequences. Dr Karl-Günther Heimöth, for instance, a doctor and psychologist who published an astrological study of homosexuality and through it became a friend of Ernst Röhm, the chief of the Sturm-Abteilung (Hitler's private army), was murdered by the Führer with Röhm and others in June 1934. The Astrological Society in Germany, on the other hand, managed to stay out of trouble, integrating with the establishment and providing a certain amount of protection for astrologers even after 1934, when the Nazis banned all 'fortune-telling', making the publication of almanacs and astrological journals illegal.

There is no evidence that Hitler himself was interested in astrology, and some evidence that he positively mistrusted it. He is often accused of having a personal astrologer, and the name most often connected with the accusation is that of Karl Ernst Krafft (1900-45). Krafft was born in

RIGHT Elspeth Ebertin, who first practised as a graphologist, became the most successful astrologer in Europe during the 1920s and 1930s. In 1917 she published in Germany her first astrological almanac, and from that time was much consulted. She was among the earliest observers to predict great power for Adolf Hitler. Her son, Reinhold Ebertin, published in 1940 his *Kombination der Gestirneinflusse*, or *Combination of Stellar Influences*, which has become one of the most important of contemporary astrological textbooks. He was the founder of the most important German astrological magazine, *Kosmobiologie*

FAR RIGHT Karl Ernst Krafft, the Swiss astrologer used by the Germans during the Second World War for the purposes of black propaganda, successfully predicted the attempt on Hitler's life in November 1939; he died on his way to Buchenwald concentration camp six years later

Switzerland, of German descent, and became a very competent astrologer. He also became a fervent admirer of Hitler, and on 2 November 1939, wrote to a Dr Fosel (then working for the RSHA, Himmler's secret intelligence service) warning that between 7 and 10 November Hitler's life would be in danger because of 'the possibility of an attempt at assassination by the use of explosive material'.

The Nazis were as disapproving of astrological predictions about the life of the head of state as the Caesars had been, and disregarded the warning. When on 9 November a bomb exploded at the Bürgerbräu beer hall in Munich minutes after Hitler had left it, Krafft could not resist sending a telegram to Rudolf Hess pointing out that he had told them so. His original letter to Fosel was dug out of the files and shown to Hitler, who passed it to Dr Goebbels. The same day, Krafft was arrested by the Gestapo and taken in for questioning. He managed to convince them that under certain circumstances such accurate predictions were possible, and was released.

In 1940, Krafft was summoned to Berlin by Goebbels to look through the prophesies of Nostradamus and translate any of them that could be used as propaganda against the Allies. It was felt that these, if dropped into unoccupied areas, might well do something to persuade the people that government by the Nazis was in the natural order of things. And indeed, after some weeks' work, Krafft claimed to have discovered verses predicting the invasion of Holland and Belgium, and foreseeing the Third Reich and the Second World War. He produced a pamphlet based on forty quatrains of Nostradamus, designed for circulation in Belgium and France, and predicting the imminent downfall of Britain. But in May of 1941, about three months later, Hess, second in command to Hitler (after Goering) flew to Scotland in an independent attempt to arrange a peace – an attempt rewarded by the Allies with over forty years' imprisonment. Martin Bormann decided that the best way of presenting the story to the German people would be to announce that Hess was actually insane, and shortly afterwards it was announced that he had been crazed by 'hypnotists, astrologers and so on'. In Britain, *The Times* actually reported that Hess had been Hitler's private astrologer!

This gave the Gestapo the excuse to clamp down on astrology in general, and those who had formerly enjoyed the protection of a sympathetic Himmler (who had arranged the release of one of their number, Wilhelm Wulff, from a concentration camp to work for him and his wife) now found themselves arrested and at worst sent to concentration camps. This delighted a number of members of the Nazi High Command, few of whom admired Himmler, and many of whom regarded him as deranged: Reinhard Heydrich, for instance, used to compare Himmler to another officer, saying 'One is worried about the stars on his epaulette, and the other about the stars in his horoscope!' Along with faith healers, clairvoyants, graphologists, Christian Scientists and spiritualists, astrologers were definitely out of favour. Krafft was among those arrested. In prison, he continued to work for a while on astrological propaganda, but at the end of 1944 caught typhus, and in January of the following year died *en route* for Buchenwald.

It is doubtful whether astrology had any effect on the German conduct of the war, despite Himmler's sympathy to it. Even Goebbels was infected, to some extent, for he sent from the besieged Berlin bunker in the last days of the war for copies of Hitler's birth chart and that of the Reich, pointing out to the Führer that both charts agreed in showing the outbreak of war and the present disastrous reverses, but also promised an overwhelming victory for Germany in April, and peace by August. Hitler preferred not to wait for the planetary change, and killed himself.

In Britain, newspaper horoscopes played a part in keeping up national morale; but the most curious British astrological story of the war is that of Louis de Wohl, a German, part-Jewish, who spent much of its duration in London, having persuaded the government, or at least some members of it, that he could tell them what advice Hitler's astrologers were giving him, and thus predict some of his plans. The venture seems to have been successful only for de Wohl, who made a lot of money from syndicated journalism, worked for the Psychological Warfare Executive's 'black propaganda' unit, and flourished a British army captain's uniform to which he was not entitled.

In America, there was the same uneasy blend of serious and popular interest in astrology as in most parts of Europe. In 1898 Luke Broughton (1828-99), an astrologer and doctor of medicine, had published his *Elements of astrology*, the first original American textbook (though it is fair to remember that Broughton had been born in Leeds, in England). And in the 1920s came the first independent American popular astrologer, Evangeline Adams (1865-1932), who leapt to popular attention after a spectacularly successful prediction of a hotel fire in New York, and for the next thirty years collected an enormous public for her syndicated columns and radio programmes (at one stage she broadcast three times a week). Her success was consolidated after a prosecution, in 1914, for fortune-telling. During the trial she was given an anonymous horoscope to interpret; on reading the result, the judge announced that the chart had been that of his son, that she was totally accurate on all points, and

BELOW Just as astrologers were freely available in the India of 1825, so in the 1980s Mr M. S. Modi works as a consultant astrologer available to guests at one of the hotels at Agra

Evangeline Adams

THE BOWL OF HEAVEN

By
EVANGELINE ADAMS

DODD, MEAD & COMPANY
NEW YORK   1926

in his view had 'raised astrology to the dignity of an exact science'. He dismissed the case.

A more serious practitioner was Dane Rudhyar (1895-   ), a distinguished composer who came to astrology through an interest in oriental music and philosophy, and believed that through astrology 'man can discover the pattern or order which reveals both his individuality and his destiny underneath or within the often seemingly chaotic and bewildering events of his personal daily existence'. His *The Planetarization of consciousness*, 1970, remains probably the most impressive astrological work to have come out of America.

Between Miss Adams and Dr Rudhyar came a multitude of other astrologers, professional and amateur. In 1960, Marcia Moore had no difficulty in finding nine hundred professional astrologers to question for a thesis she was writing; in 1969 one journalist estimated that over ten

Evangeline Adams, the best-known American astrologer of her generation, and the first to turn broadcasting to her advantage thousand Americans were making a living from astrology (probably the majority of them by making predictions that would be mistrusted by more serious astrologers).

The incursion of astrology into the popular press was pioneered in London as recently as 1930 by R. H. Naylor (1889–1952). He was invited by the editor of *The Sunday Express* to cast the horoscope of the newly born Princess Margaret Rose, daughter of the future King George VI. He did so, not only outlining in his article a character now recognizably that of the Princess, but predicting that 'events of tremendous importance to the Royal Family and the nation will come about near her seventh year'. Unforeseen events indeed resulted in her father's accession to the throne a few months before her seventh birthday.

But more important for astrology, the newspaper's editor invited Mr Naylor to contribute another article to the following week's issue; and in it he suggested that British aircraft might be in danger. On the very day of publication, the airship R-101 crashed in northern France. The newspaper gave Mr Naylor massive publicity, and he became famous overnight. Since then no popular newspaper or magazine has been able to escape the necessity to publish regular astrological forecasts for its readers.

Recently, astrologers have managed to persuade editors to allow them to make use of and mention various planets and their possible effects on readers' lives; but it was Naylor who invented the Sun sign column. He had to find a way of writing so that each reader could feel involved, and chose to divide his essays into twelve paragraphs, one for each person born when the Sun was passing through a particular zodiac sign. This is by no means a predominantly important part of astrological forecasting, but it is one recognizable by every reader, because it depends on the day, rather than the precise time, of birth. Unrelenting concentration on the Sun sign has done untold damage to astrology, for even those who claim to be intelligent critics are often under the impression that astrologers base serious character analyses on this single aspect of a birth chart.

Journalists often write of a booming interest in astrology – by which they mean, on the whole, the growth of an almost entirely superstitious interest in the subject. There was a time, in the 1960s and 1970s, when you only had to sit next to a stranger on a plane, or stand next to someone at a party, to be asked 'What's your sign?' In those days, the Sun sign was almost the only element of a birth chart to be known. This left the field open for 'astrologers' who were really clairvoyants. Maurice Woodruff, the Englishman who numbered so many international film stars among his clients (Peter Sellers, for one, hardly made a move without consulting him) was much more clairvoyant than astrologer. In America, Carroll Righter was more conventional, but probably no less uncritically consulted – by among others a film star called Ronald Reagan, whose publicly expressed interest in astrology has recently diminished.

Those who consulted Woodruff or Righter would have been unlikely to have heard of Dane Rudhyar or of John Addey (1920–82), the Englishman whose advanced work on what he termed 'the harmonics of cosmic periods' is believed by many astrologers to be crucial. In some areas of the world there was a more informed wide interest: in the east, especially, where Mrs Indira Gandhi has never disguised her trust. Nor have many prominent Indian politicians and public servants, despite a far more fatalistic astrology than is acceptable in the west. In Sri Lanka, astrology plays a prominent part in public affairs.

In general, prejudice seems to be the only factor to stand in the way of a serious scientific consideration of the astrological theory. In private, even the most sceptical of critics may admit to a suspicion that not enough examination has been made of the available facts, despite the availability of statistical evidence on a large scale. Until fairly recently, such evidence has been prepared by astrologers themselves, and has thus been open to criticism. But equally, critics have been unprepared even to look at that evidence, or indeed to make any real attempt to understand what it is that they criticize. Some three years ago, two hundred scientists at a European convention issued a statement warning the public that belief in astrology was futile and could be dangerous. When questioned, it was found that the great majority of them believed that astrologers worked only on the basis of the position of the Sun at the time of birth. (It is ironical that their warning, better expressed, would have been supported by most astrologers, as concerned at uncritical belief in Sun-sign astrology as anyone!) Neither has it been publicised that a greater number declined to sign the statement than put their names to it.

Some scientists are able even to ignore 'astrological' facts that turn up, unprompted, in their own fields. Surgeons provide statistics which relate a difficulty in stopping bleeding during surgical operations at certain phases of the Moon, and doctors at blood transfusion centres note with surprise that donors bleed more freely when the Moon is full. Tell them that ancient astrologers pointed this out, and they are dumbfounded. Meteorologists announce that there seems to be a correlation between the position of certain planets and events on the surface of the Sun which the weather, but assert that this has nothing to do with astrology.

Occasionally, however, those with absolutely no interest in the subject

John Addey, the most
distinguished British
astrologer of the second
half of the twentieth
century, whose theory of
the 'harmonics of cosmic
periods' is crucial to
modern astrological
thought

are sufficiently intrigued to involve themselves. The most notable of these
is perhaps the French statistician Michel Gauquelin, assisted by his wife
Françoise. Gauquelin's interest was prompted by his decision to check
the statistics on which Krafft based his *Treatise on astrobiology*, published in the 1930s. With the help of a computer, Gauquelin showed that
these were improperly correlated. But certain interesting facts emerged
from them, nevertheless, and Gauquelin decided to test two of them – the
propositions that people born during 'odd' months of the year were
introverts, while those born during 'even' months were extraverts. This
seemed obviously one of those lunatic traditional astrological propositions that could not, in a sensible world, be believed. To his amazement
and irritation, Gauquelin found that his computers confirmed it (as far as
introversion and extraversion are measureable).

To summarize, Gauquelin went on to examine the birth charts of thousands of sportsmen, actors and scientists chosen on the basis of their success in their professions. Statistically, sportsmen tended to be born when the planet Mars was, astrologically, dominant; actors under Jupiter; scientists and doctors under Saturn. Gauquelin's propositions have been re-examined by Hans Eysenck, who agrees with them.

There have been other incidental illustrations of the astrological proposition. Maki Takata has examined the effect of sunspot activity on the flocculation index (the rate at which blood albumin curdles) and found a close relationship; Giorgio Piccardi has shown that both sunspots and the Moon's cycle affect various chemical reactions; Y. Rocard has recently shown that men and women have a very delicate sensitivity to the earth's magnetic field – the sense homing pigeons use to find their way back to their lofts over many miles of countryside. All this has a very obvious relationship to astrology, as have more obvious correlations of planetary movements and events on earth (such as the example of John H. Nelson's work in meteorology, see p. 157).

In recent years some astrologers have made great efforts to look critically and coolly at their work; a lengthy book, *Recent Advances in Natal Astrology* (1977; a second edition is in preparation) related both successes and failures, sought out false propositions, astrological legends, badly devised and conducted 'experiments' and unsupported claims with such rigour and objectivity that many astrologers condemned it as an attack on their craft. Far from that, it is an almost unique attempt to look seriously at the subject and to examine it critically but not dismissively. There are relatively few areas of astrology which it suggests are worth thoughtful and constructive examination (though these are widely spread, and include the Sun-sign elements as well as more arcane theories). As the authors, Geoffrey Dean and Arthur Mather, put it:

> In recent years properly controlled experiments have failed to sustain many of astrology's claims, and have shown beyond doubt that much of its apparent validity can be explained by the demonstrable gullibility of practitioners and clients alike ... On the other hand the same experiments have revealed that not all is fallacious. Enough remains that cannot be explained by gullibility or coincidence to justify further study.

No one who has seriously looked at the evidence (and a great deal of evidence now exists) could argue with that.

Progress is being made. The Astrological Association in Britain and the American Federation of Astrologers hold annual conferences as well as weekly meetings; certainly theories are aired that seem decidedly 'chintzy', but a great deal of serious work is also done. *Correlation*, a

Geoffrey Dean and
Arthur Mather at work
on the production of
*Recent Advances in
Natal Astrology* (1977)
a dispassionate and
critical examination
of modern astrological
theory

Tom Shanks operates a
Prime Computer in San
Diego, California, the
biggest computer
dedicated full time to
astrology. It will
calculate a whole birth-
chart in less than two
seconds

A Conference at the Institute of Psychiatry in London in 1981 attracted delegates from many countries. LEFT *to* RIGHT at the dinner-table are: Jacob Venker (Holland), Dr David Nias (UK), Dr Michel Gauquelin (France), Simon Best (New Zealand, Editor of *Correlation*), Prof. Alan Smithers (UK), Tom Shanks (USA, Astro Computing Services), John Addey (UK), Austin Levy (Australia, Astrosearch), Jacques Halbronn (France, Mouvement Astrologique Unifié)

regular journal published by the Astrological Association, is probably the most serious periodical in the history of the subject. In London within the past year as many as four hundred astrologers and students met for an evening's study, on a serious level; and there are regular meetings and conferences in most western countries, many of them international. The British Faculty of Astrological Studies holds classes in London and has a correspondence course which has been taken by students in most countries of the world. Its final examination involves several papers, and there is a high and rigorous standard of marking, with relatively few passes each year.

Yes, Sun-sign books continue to be published, and account for the majority of sales of astrological books. But many of them now have tables of planetary positions which enable the reader to work out a virtually complete horoscope. Historians too are beginning to explore the documents left by the astrologers of the past. Even science begins to show a reluctant interest through the study of various natural rhythms, of cosmobiology, and of correlations of terrestrial events and planetary movements. It seems likely that the next fifty years or so will make it clear to what extent the longest-living scientific tradition is based on superstition, and to what extent it can help to illuminate the nature of our existence.

A BRIEF GLOSSARY

angle, in See *aspect*

ascendant The ascendant sign is the sign of the Zodiac rising over the eastern horizon at a specific time; an individual's 'ascending sign' is thus the sign rising at the moment of his or her birth.

aspect The angle made by a line drawn from one planet to the centre of the earth, and a line from another to the same point.

astrolabe An instrument formerly used in astronomy for taking the altitudes of stars or planets.

birth-chart A chart showing the positions of the Sun, Moon and planets as they would be seen at the moment of one's birth, from the place of birth.

chiromancy The divination of character and future events from the markings on the palm of the hand; 'palmistry'.

conjunction Two or more planets which appear, when seen from earth, to occupy the same or almost the same position in the sky are said to be 'in conjunction.'

decan A section made up of ten of the thirty degrees into which a Zodiacal sign is divided.

ecliptic The apparent path of the Sun around the earth.

Enuma Anu Enlil A series of over 7000 astrological omens collected together at the time of the first dynasty of Babylon, c 1830–1531 BC.

ephemeris (*pl ephemerides*) A publication or publications containing the positions of the Sun, Moon and planets at noon or midnight GMT for every day of any particular year or years.

geomancy Divination from figures made by joining together a number of dots made on paper at random.

horoscope Properly, a *birth-chart* (cf), but the term now popularly used to denote a characterisation or forecast made by the study of the birth-chart. Because of its 'fortune-telling' connotations, the term is unpopular with astrologers. A *judicial horoscope* in modern times refers to forecasts made about an entire country; similarly, *mundane astrology*. In *horary astrology* an astrologer will set up a chart for the moment a question is asked, and claim to provide an answer on the basis of that chart. An astrologer will use *electional astrology* to select a propitious moment for some future action.

houses, the Twelve traditional divisions of the astrological birth-chart arrived at by calculation from the birth data. Each house traditionally affects a different area of life. There are various systems of house division.

mithraeum A temple to the Persian god identified with the Sun. His cult spread through Europe with the Romans, whose emperors supported it because it supported the divine rights of monarchs.

mul.APIN tablets The most famous series of Babylonian astronomical tablets, written in about 700 BC, but containing material collected as early as 1300.

precession of the equinoxes The movement of the point of vernal equinox along the ecliptic at the rate of about 50 seconds of longitude each year.

stele An upright slab bearing an inscription or other carving.

synastry The comparison of two or more charts of individuals.

synchronicity The term coined by the psychologist C. G. Jung to describe certain apparently inexplicable coincidences.

zodiac, sidereal and tropical The ancients used the sidereal or 'constellational' zodiac, arbitrarily divided into twelve signs of thirty degrees, starting at Aries O°. Most modern astrologers regard this as illogical, and use the 'tropical' zodiac, which begins at the intersection of the ecliptic and the equator at the Spring equinox.

A BRIEF BIBLIOGRAPHY

The following is a check-list of some interesting books bearing on the history of astrology, both by astrologers and non-astrologers, all published within the last two hundred years. Many earlier books – from Ptolemy to William Lilly – are available in modern editions and translations, but have been omitted for reasons of space.

Adams, Evangeline *Your Place in the Sun* (1928)

Addey, John M. *Harmonics in Astrology* (1976)

Barlow, T. D. *The Medieval World Picture* (1950)

Baughan, J. *Influence of the Stars* (1897)

Capp Bernard *Astrology and the Popular Press* (1979)

Carter, Charles *An Encyclopaedia of Psychological Astrology* (1963).

Cockayne, T. O. *Leechdoms and Starcraft of Early England* (1864)

Coopland, G. W. *Oresme and the Astrologers* (1952)

Copenhaver, Brian P. *Symphorien Champier* (1978)

Cumont, F. *Astrology and Religion among the Romans* (1912)

Dean, Geoffrey, and Mather, Arthur *Recent Advances in Natal Astrology* (1977).

de Wohl, Louis *Secret Service of the Sky* (ND)

Ebertin, Reinhold *The Combination of Stellar Influences* (1972)

Ellis, Keith *Prediction and Prophesy* (1973)

Eysenck, Hans, and Nias, D. K. B. *Astrology: Science or Superstition?* (1982)

Fowler, A. D. S. *Spenser and the Numbers of Time* (1964).

Gauquelin, Michel *The Cosmic Clocks* (1967)

– *The Scientific Basis of Astrology* (1969)

– *Cosmic Influences On Human Behaviour* (1973)

Gleadow, Rupert *The Origin of the Zodiac* (1968)

– *Your Character in the Zodiac* (1968)

Hartmann, F. *Astrological Geomancy* (1889)

Howe, Ellic *Raphael, or the Royal Merlin* (1964)

– *Nostradamus and the Nazis* (1965)

– *Urania's children* (1967)

– *The Black Game* (1982)

Jaquin, N. *Theory of Metaphysical Influence* (1958)

Jung, C. G. *Synchronicity: an Acausal Connecting Principle* (1955)

– *Alchemical Studies* (1960)

Kenton, Warren *Astrology, the Celestial Mirror* (1974)

Koestler, Arthur *The Sleepwalkers* (1959)

Leventhal, Herbert *In the Shadow of the Enlightenment* (1976)

Lindsay, Jack *Origins of Astrology* (1971)

MacNeice, Louis *Astrology* (1964)

Mayo, Jeff *Teach Yourself Astrology* (1968)

Mercier, C. A. *Astrology in Medicine* (1914)

Michell, John F. C. *The View Over Atlantis* (1969)

Naylor, Phyllis *Astrology: an Historical Examination* (1967)

Neugebauer, O. E., and Van Hoesel, H. B. *Greek Horoscopes* (1959)

Palgrave, F. *Astrology and Alchemy* (1922)

Parker, Derek *The Question of Astrology* (1970)

– *Familiar to all: William Lilly and Astrology in the 17th century* (1975)

Parker, Derek and Julia *The Compleat Astrologer* (1971)

Pingree, David *Political Horoscopes from the Reign of Zeno* (1976)

Plomer, H. R. *English Almanacs and Almanac-makers of the 16th and 17th centuries* (ND)

Rowse, A. L. *Simon Forman* (1974)

Russell, Eric *Astrology and Prediction* (1972)

Saxl, F. *Revival of Antique Astrology* (1957)

Simmonite, W. J. *Complete Arcana of Astrology* (1890)

Thierens, Adolph E. *Elements of Esoteric Astrology* (1931)

Thomas, Keith *Religion and the Decline of Magic* (1971)

Thorndike, Lynn *The History of Magic and Experimental Science* (1941)

Tillyard, E. M. W. *The Elizabethan World Picture* (1943)

Walker, D. P. *Spiritual and Demonic Magic from Ficino to Campanella* (1958)

Wedel, T. O. *Medical Attitude to Astrology* (1920)

Wulf, Wilhelm *Zodiac and Swastika* (1973)

Zinner, D. *Stars Above Us* (1957)

INDEX